BY MOURNING TONGUES

BY MOURNING TONGUES

TONGUES

Studies in English Elegy

ERIC SMITH

'*By mourning tongues*
The death of the poet was kept from his poems.'
(W. H. Auden, 'In Memory of W. B. Yeats')

BOYDELL PRESS . ROWMAN AND LITTLEFIELD

© Eric Smith 1977

First published 1977

Published by The Boydell Press, P.O. Box 24, Ipswich IP1 1JJ
and Rowan and Littlefield, 81 Adams Drive, Totowa, N.J. 07512

ISBN (UK) 0 85115 075 6

Library of Congress Cataloging in Publication Data

Smith, Eric, 1940–
  By mourning tongues.

  Includes bibliographical references and index.
  1. Elegiac poetry, English–History and
criticism.   I.   Title.
PR509.E4S6   821'.04   77-1728
ISBN 0-87471-939-9

The jacket illustration is Churchyard at Stoke Poges
by John Constable, reproduced by permission of
the Victoria and Albert Museum

Printed in Great Britain by
Richard Clay (The Chaucer Press), Ltd,
Bungay, Suffolk

CONTENTS

Introduction

   I The Context   1

  II Milton – *Lycidas*   22

 III Gray – *Elegy Written in a Country Churchyard*   40

 IV Shelley – *Adonais*   55

  V Arnold – *The Scholar-Gipsy* and *Thyrsis*   79

 VI Tennyson – *In Memoriam*   100

    Notes   135

    Index   145

INTRODUCTION

'The elegy is a form practised by almost every poet, and nothing is more revealing than to examine it in the hands of different writers.'[1] This book is a critical discussion of major English elegies. Of these, *Lycidas* is most closely related to formal pastoral elegy. But, as we see it now, genre is not a static thing, and pastoral elegy as a literary form indeed evolved in a highly accretive fashion over nearly two thousand years, accompanied by much theoretical debate as to what might or might not be included under its head.[2]

Of the more or less formal genre, *Lycidas* is in English poetry the climax. After it, elegy and pastoral generally might be said to have declined.[3] Perhaps it would be more accurate to say that, in the longer term, they became diffused. They were produced in quantity throughout the Eighteenth Century, but with little feeling or conviction. But from half way through the Century the bookish reproduction of scenes, and the well-worn personifications which had come to supplement the classical pantheon, began to be replaced by increasingly realistic description, of 'nature'[4] and also of true rural society. The general moral of the 'transient smile of Fate', which Dyer (in *Grongar Hill*, 1726) draws from the fashionable contemplation of ruins, appears to be tagged on in part to excuse the detailed description of a real place (rather than the classical 'imitation') as a subject for poetry – though, if we did not know otherwise, we could hardly distinguish the actual 'prospect' from an imaginary portrayal of 'the purple grove, Haunt of Phyllis, Queen of Love'. Gray's *Elegy* (1750) incorporates more thoroughly a somewhat similar 'moral' but following on detailed description which does not require such a defence. The description of the village in Goldsmith's *Deserted Village* (1750) is felt to be entirely justified by, is indeed part of, his theme of the desolation of local communities. Meanwhile, the pastoral elegy as such is for a while overshadowed by the lucubrations of the 'graveyard poets' (notably Blair's *The Grave* (1743) and Young's *Night Thoughts* (1742–5)) whose obsession, though it enlarged elegiac resources, was not immediately adaptable to sincere elegy. But gradually during the Century there emerges an association of reflection upon universal problems, including mortality, with the realistic painting of rural scenery. The association means that the 'realism' is in fact tinted with a series of implied qualities – sublimity, humility, truth, spirituality, and so on – which may be brought to the mind of the beholder or be held to be inherent in Nature.

Pastoral, for English poets, is essentially a disguise. For whatever reason, people are dressed up as shepherds. But, though there may be a sense of approaching the fundamental verities in Nature, 'nature' and rural life in poetry may also be a disguise, either because they may constitute an avoidance of uncomfortable reality, or because they may be adopted for a deliberate translation of that reality into a seemingly simple world uncomplicated by contingencies of everyday life. *The Scholar-Gipsy* and *Thyrsis* indicate the difficulties of believing 'nature' is more real than pastoral. *In Memoriam* indicates the turning sour of the idea of fundamental verities, as indeed of the Romantic exaltation of Nature, although it achieves a working adjustment to a Nature less benign and idyllic.

I think it must be felt that the poems after *Lycidas* draw on *Lycidas* and with it are part of an unbroken stream of poetry linking pastoral or 'nature' with elegy. There is a broad continuity from Theocritus and the author of the *Lament for Bion*, through Virgil, Marot, Castiglione and Petrarch, and on to Spenser, Milton, Shelley, Arnold and Tennyson – on indeed to Auden, whose highly conscious rejection of the tradition for his *In Memory of W. B. Yeats* (1939) invokes, as it were by inversion, familiar themes and images. I have set out to suggest this continuity.

With Gray's *Elegy* the matter is, and perhaps always will be, debatable. It stands apart from the main English elegies; yet any list of them would seem deficient if it were omitted. Even if the possible personal promptings for the poem could be proved to have led to it (which seems unlikely) their proper place in the reading of the poem would remain uncertain. It does, however, incorporate important aspects of the tradition, and the fact that it might so very easily have certainly belonged to the tradition has seemed to me sufficient grounds for including it here.

Chapter I examines in broad terms both the themes and formal considerations in the tradition. Thereafter, discussion is chronological, with the exception that Arnold is placed before Tennyson. The exception is made partly because Arnold's shorter pieces, and *Thyrsis* in particular, are closely related to earlier pastoral elegy as more strictly seen, and are structurally closer to *Adonais*, and partly because *In Memoriam* is in some respects more 'modern' and, in its larger scope, the natural conclusion.

ACKNOWLEDGEMENTS

The poems considered here are among the most read and most discussed in the language, learnt by rote maybe when 'ignorance is bliss', revisited with new comprehension 'in the vale of years', and constantly lived with meanwhile. I am aware of owing a large debt to many previous writers about them, but conscious that the debt must be bigger than I can now identify. Some such sources are mentioned in the Notes, but generally these authors are too numerous to name, and it is not easy to distinguish conscious influence from development born of an agreement unregistered at the time. Quirks and errors I of course accept as my own.

I owe a more particular debt to certain people; to Brian Taylor formerly, and to Graham Midgley presently, of St. Edmund Hall, Oxford; to J. I. M. Stewart of Christ Church, Oxford; to John Lawlor of the University of Keele; to my father and to my wife, for interest and forbearance. I know that they have affected the content of this book more deeply and less definably than those whose presence may be acknowledged in chapter and verse, more deeply, indeed, than they themselves may recognise. At the same time, they bear no responsibility for its faults.

I

The Context

Pastoral and Elegy

In a previous study[1] I considered important versions of the story of the Fall of Man in English Literature. One point which emerged was the increasing personalisation in modern times of what in earlier versions had been an impersonal myth from which the concerns of the writer, whilst no doubt embodied, did not explicitly emerge. The present discussion follows a somewhat similar direction.

The journey from the Fall of Man to pastoral and pastoral elegy is not a long one. The themes are interconnected and alike of central human concern. Indeed, the interrelation of the Fall and pastoral has received penetrating comment.[2] So far as the Christian tradition goes, the pastoral world is a sort of Eden. It may be a more or less accurately conceived preferable world of past history, or it may be a utopia to come if certain large difficulties of the present can be surmounted. Again, it may be a world which can only be gained, or in essence regained, by transcending the human condition as we know it. But, whilst it may be the Eden from which man fell and which he may hope to regain, it looks back further than the Christian tradition and in particular to the classical myth of the Golden Age.

On the other hand – and this Professor Empson has well brought out[3] – the pastoral world may be less an ideal to be captured or recaptured than a simplification, a sample society where what are thought to be the fundamental issues of living together are brought out and discussed away from the temporal and incidental distractions of the present, a world where the pretensions of social hierarchy can be mocked with a measure of impunity by the uncluttered mind of the inspired idiot. Or, if we are not with a levelled society, in pastoral we are close to Natural forces, to death the leveller. The 'inevitable hour' (Gray's *Elegy* 35) awaits high and low alike, and 'great and mean meet massed in death' (*Adonais* 185). Or again, it was debated by Puttenham, Webbe, and others, following classical sources, whether pastoral must have been the first poetry. Certainly it is idealised (somewhat ironically, in view of its artificial development) for showing the poet naturally related to his society and having a useful function, being engaged in seclusion in a fundamentally significant act of 'making' (as depicted in Marvell's *The Garden*). But, whatever aspect is to the fore, the pastoral world is essentially a world apart. It is offered, implicitly or explicitly, for consideration alongside the real world of the writer and his public, with a feeling that the real world falls short. The pastoral represents, or at least suggests, what is missing.

In this context elegy is a particular sort of pastoral, for elegy is specifically about what is missing and also about what is more certainly known to have been formerly possessed. It is a crucial and intimate human situation removed, very often, to the abstracted world of pastoral. What is missing may be a particular person or a particular quality of life, or it may be both. Where elegy and pastoral are closely linked, the conventional pastoralism of the Golden Age and of Sicily as portrayed by Theocritus (most probably from Alexandria, thereby inaugurating the nostalgia and artifice of pastoral) represents an ideal world to which the lost beloved is felt to have belonged. It is not necessary to believe that such a world actually existed, only that it embodies elements of an ideal which did exist and ought now to exist. Where, on the other hand, personal loss predominates, the beloved appears in a setting more rural than pastoral, a countryside (now possibly ruined by enclosure, the plough, or development) whose details we may even be able to identify. The passing of such a countryside, with its accompanying social order, may also be the subject of lament.

It is one apparent paradox of the Fall that it has its compensation. The subsequent and possibly consequent redemption by Christ may appear so overwhelming a benefit as almost to deny that the Fall was a fall at all. As Milton's Adam wonders,

> full of doubt I stand
> Whether I should repent me now of sin
> By me done and occasioned, or rejoyce
> Much more, that much more good thereof shall spring.
>
> (*Paradise Lost* xii 473–6)

Elegy, where it includes consolation, has a related conundrum. When, by way of consolation, the apotheosis of the beloved, or the prospect of jumping the hateful boundary between life and death so as to make renewed contact, is the final triumphant impression, human life is liable to be diminished. The passing of sorrow obstinately seems to be the death of love. Moreover, we are inclined to feel that, however superlative is the future depicted, whatever the nature of reunion, it remains but an individual's vision (and this even in the manifestly Christian consolation) peculiarly dependent on the verbal art which creates it. The 'poetry' is a sort of self-deception, plausible while it lasts, but making perhaps unreasonable demands upon us. We seem to be invited not only to enter a pastoral world very different from the chair in which we are sitting, but also to join in an act of faith.

Elegy of this sort will profit from a 'dramatic' reading, which has perhaps not always been sufficiently given to it in the past; the characters, indeed the speaker himself, are fictional characters not identified with the poet and having no designs upon us. Yet nonetheless, at its best it still provokes and disturbs. It will not permit us to leave at the back of our minds the questions which it raises. In the English tradition at least, there is a contrast between the idyllic pastoral and the intrusive reality, between both these and whatever consolation may be found, a contrast which can make us uncomfortable both as human beings and as critics.

Attitudes to Time

'Time the destroyer is time the preserver.'[4] Elegy is a battle with and also an acknowledgement of time, and time appears in elegy in several ways. Primarily, time is transience, represented by the fact of death, both of the beloved and of the forms of Nature around. But time we know also to be a healer, and on this the poet has to tread warily, for the healing must be felt to be more than the mere passing of grief into indifference and forgetfulness. Time is a seemingly interminable interval before the lover and beloved are, in the conventional phrase, united in death – which may be a blessed reunion or at the least a cessation of sorrow. Time is also that which takes away, in its apparently 'healing' aspect, even that (grief, memory) of the beloved which, to the subjectively minded, may yet appear to survive on earth.

It is a feature of grief that it involves identification with that which is lost in the effort to avert a change which in reality has already occurred. This identification may go far beyond any which existed in real life and be complicated with a sense of guilt at former inadequacy.[5] Such a development is particularly apparent in post-Romantic elegies where for religious reasons the concentration on an afterlife to which the mourner moves, anticipating reunion, may not be available. Such poetry often concentrates, in what appears to be the artistic correlative of the process of identification in real life, on the precise recollection of associated scenes and events. A moving and well-known instance is *Poems of 1912–13*, where Hardy recreates with loving precision scenes of his earlier life with his first

3

wife Emma.[6] The purpose is an insistence on integrity and the survival of the relationship after one of the partners is dead;

> *I see what you are doing: you are leading me on*
> *To the spots we knew when we haunted here together . . .*

> *Trust me, I mind not, though life lours,*
> *The bringing me here; nay, bring me here again!*
> *I am just the same as when*
> *Our days were a joy and our paths through flowers.*

We may note something similar in Arnold's *Thyrsis*, both in the discovery that the recollected scenes, with their frequent allusions to those set out more fully in *The Scholar-Gipsy*, are 'gone', hedges and flowers flattened by 'the ploughboy's team', and also in the revelation, valued above all else, that the 'signal-elm' is still there, guaranteeing continuity with the world of the former poem, with Clough and with whatever linked them of old.

Re-creation, the product of grief, is both a homage to the departed and also an assertion of his or her continued existence in the mind of the bereaved. Yet, as is tautly observed in *Adonais*, it is the final irony of Time that, whether or not it is desirable, grief itself cannot live. If it lives in the individual, that is not to say that it will live in his successor:

> *Alas that all we loved of him should be,*
> *But for our grief, as if it had not been,*
> *And grief itself be mortal! Woe is me!*

$$(181-3)$$

The subjective immortality, the last resort of the sceptic in the face of death, is not in any vital sense available. Time, as it 'heals', also destroys what it 'preserves', and only some concept of an afterlife can survive the onslaught. During *In Memoriam* Tennyson seems to intend to show just this passing of a stultifying grief and the substitution of a transcendent consolation. It was at first a question of preserving love by grief ('Let love clasp grief, lest both be drowned' – i). The 'measure' of his grief was a substitute for specific praise of Hallam (lxxv). But slowly he arrives at the perception already noted in *Adonais* – 'O last regret, regret can die' (lxxviii). By the end of the poem, grief is rejected – indeed he shows himself freed of it to such an extent as, for some readers, to call in question the feelings that have gone before; 'regret' is dead but, by virtue of the complex consolation which he has evolved, 'love is more Than in the summers that are flown', and he himself has 'grown To something greater than before' (*Epilogue*). Yet, although re-creation, fixation in grief, can buy immortality for the beloved only at the cost of the mourner's vitality and health, grief remains an important and perhaps never convincingly

4

defeated element in elegy, being in some sense a guarantee and replica of love.

The Role of Nature

There is a close connection between pastoral and personal elegy, and that arises from the evident fact that pastoral, however artificial it became in its conventions, fundamentally represented a basic life in contact with Nature. And, through all the nymphs and naiads, the jovial rays of Phoebus and the realms of Flora and of Pan, this aspect stands out. What we have is a minimal society in proximity to the elemental forces, and their unconscious manifestations, which govern man in all his social relations and all aspects of his conscious being. The perpetual concern is the relationship of man as thinking and possibly spiritual being to this world. Of course, the undistraught spectator will by and large assess this relationship as one of kinship on the physical side and of separation on the conscious or spiritual side, and settle for man as being between animal and angel. He will also observe that man cannot be identified with what he can, in uncertain measure, control and organise to his own advantage.

Death and bereavement, however, appear to upset such a balance and also the balance or equivocation of viewpoint. The dissolution of the body brings to the forefront that side of man which is in the grip of the elemental forces whose purposes, compared with those which a conscious man may set himself, are so obscure. The fact that dissolution in turn feeds the earth which will provide for, among other things, future conscious beings, does little to palliate the apparent futility of the proceedings:

> *The leprous corpse, touched by this spirit tender,*
> *Exhales itself in flowers of tender breath;*
> *Like incarnations of the stars, when splendour*
> *Is changed to fragrance, they illumine death*
> *And mock the merry worm that wakes beneath;*
> *Nought we know, dies. Shall that alone which knows*
> *Be as a sword consumed before the sheath*
> *By sightless lightning?*

> (*Adonais* 171–9)

The one thing which appears to be exempt from rebirth is conscious being. Thus the conservation of Nature's store in endless cycles is not calculated to inspire confidence in the immortality, the eternal significance, of the individual.

It is the impinging of animal and vegetable life on human life which draws together Nature, 'pastoral' (as Nature in a conventional and refined form) and elegy – the observation, made pressing by experience of death,

5

that in vital and perhaps quintessential respects man is one with the animals and the trees. Here may be, as the elegists remind us, comfort, for spring cannot be far behind winter and if Natural seasons are reborn, why should humankind be exempt from the process? That comfort is, however, an illusion soon surrendered for, in Western poetry at least, the possibility of a series of rebirths moving towards no end is a possibility of endless separation from the beloved, an eternity without the finality of perfection to make it acceptable. The prospect appears to be of an unearthly game of tag:

> *Yet oft when sundown skirts the moor*
> *An inner trouble I behold,*
> *A spectral doubt which makes me cold,*
> *That I shall be thy mate no more,*
>
> *Though following with an upward mind*
> *The wonders that have come to thee,*
> *Through all the secular world to-be,*
> *But ever more a life behind.*

(*In Memoriam* xli)[8]

On the other hand, when the forces linking man and Nature are so powerful, that which is apparently unique in Nature, namely man's individual soul, draws the two apart and becomes, of course, the main road in the search for lasting compensation for the blow which Nature has dealt. The distinction is indeed problematic for, whilst abundant metaphor (of stormy passions and the like) embodies an analogy between elemental facts and human feelings, and whilst human emotions have from time to time been ascribed to bodily causes (the humours, or chemical imbalance in the brain, in the more modern version), the mood of the bereaved may offer evidence of a striking disjunction between the two; in the classical trope, spring comes but there is only a deep winter in the mind and that winter corresponds to death. (It is the paradox of the immortal grief again, which cannot be immortality.) In a setting close to Nature, such a disjunction emphasises the incomprehensibility of death. Thus,

> *No joy the blowing season gives,*
> *The herald melodies of spring...*

(*In Memoriam* xxxviii)

Or, in a non-elegiac context where there is prospect of relief by prayer,

> *See, banks and brakes*
> *Now leavéd thick! lacéd they are again*
> *With fretty chervil, look, and fresh wind shakes*
> *Them; birds build – but not I build; no; but strain,*

6

Time's eunuch, and not breed one work that wakes.
Mine, O thou Lord of Life, send my roots rain.[9]

When mood and season coincide, the one is a reinforcement of the other – the mourner allies himself with that power he is trying to fathom, and 'pathetic fallacy' in one form or another may arise, as in the recurrent image of Nature mourning, in season or out of season;

> *Ay me that dreerie death should strike so mortall stroke*
> *That can undoe Dame natures kindly course;*
> *The faded lockes fall from the loftie oke,*
> *The flouds do gaspe, for dryed is theyr sourse,*
> *And flouds of teares flowe in theyr stead perforse.*
> *The mantled medowes mourne,*
> *Theyr sondry colours tourne . . .*[10]

or, with a close debt to the Greek *Lament for Bion,*

> *Grief made the young Spring wild, and she threw down*
> *Her kindling buds, as if she autumn were,*
> *Or they dead leaves; since her delight is flown,*
> *For whom should she have waked the sullen year?*

(*Adonais* 136–9)

In the criticism of 'pathetic fallacy' one can go too far too easily. It is obvious, I think, that no-one ever believed all this about a sudden devastation following on a sad death. From a resemblance of spring to human joy, and of autumn to human woe, the sense of analogy was fancifully extended until Nature was animated and would even depart, out of human sympathy, from that very seasonal pattern which produced the anology in the first place. Yet, if the fancy was not believed, it could only spring from a deep sense of kinship between man and Nature for whom alike the fact of death did not appear to make sense. 'Fallacy' of this sort springs out of basic human needs. The feeling of kinship may or may not linger with us from a more primitive stage of existence, but what it does powerfully suggest is what appears to the bereaved (and to others at times) as the essential loneliness of man in the face of forces which appear to make a mockery of all that he holds valuable.

In the mourning of Nature there is an assumption that a man's mood normally bears some relation to the moods of Nature collected under the heads of the seasons. But there is another way in which Nature is repeatedly assumed to follow the human pattern or, conversely (for the matter is fundamental and never resolved), in which man is assumed to parallel and perhaps to be controlled by the course of Nature. This is, of course, in the conception of human life as one big year, ending in the sere

7

of winter, with some prospect of eternal spring elsewhere. In the great elegies it is largely an assumption against which the exceptions are viewed, since normally these subjects are dead ere their prime – or, as *In Memoriam* (xxiv) succinctly puts it, 'thy leaf has perished in the green'. They die preternaturally young in years and their demise appears all the more unjust because their potentialities far exceeded the average. Because so often they were men, they seemed (in the assumption of the times) to have before them the chance of achievement and fame, and in this respect they are identified with their poets' own problems as women could not have been. There is in these elegies a bewilderment and at times an anger that the 'big year' analogy does not hold good, that human life does not run the course apparently indicated by Nature.

By way of contrast, consider a superb elegy – the equal in quality, but not in range, of any discussed here – on the death of the poet's wife. Henry King's *Exequy upon His Wife*, while it has a number of typical features, does not explore the range of problems or involve so passionate a sense of injustice and waste as is characteristic of the elegy on the poet (or anyone whose calling is importantly akin to that of the poet). For similar reasons, no doubt, and also because what is involved is Eros rather than friendship or even acquaintance, it has a unique tenderness to it. It was an 'untimely fate'. King sees it in terms of the big day rather than of the big year – 'overcast Before thou hadst thy noon-tide past' and 'Thou scarce hadst seen so many years As day tells hours' – and his consolation is that every day and night brings him nearer to the union of souls in an undoubted afterlife; the poem becomes as it were a slow-march towards that moment:

> But hark! my pulse, like a soft drum,
> Beats my approach, tells thee I come;
> And slow howe'er my marches be
> I shall at last sit down by thee.

This is profoundly moving. But it is not an emotion found in the elegies discussed in this book, for they do not, with the possible exception of *In Memoriam*, speak of or pretend to speak of love, and they are not happy (or faithful) to wait for the big year to conclude its course. If reunion is sought, it is sought partly for the principle's sake (this is evidence in *Adonais*), for the triumph over transience. Or it is sought as relief to personal suffering, or for the guarantee that there are values, contrary to the appearance of brute Nature and the larger power of which brute Nature is agent, values closely related to the poet and his function. So there is especial point in the imagery of the seasons. The pastoral world is an apparently immutable order, the established setting of the poem which is knocked awry by untimely death. Pastoral has its idealised society and its daily routines of taking sheep out, feeding them, herding them back at sundown, or of drawing in the plough at the appropriate hour.[11] But the pastoral, like the real world, is subject to the storms and the seas, and those storms can be metaphorical as well as real. Whether we call it 'nature' or 'pastoral', wherever the walls may appear to be, there is always that beyond it in terms of which it appears less than the ultimate power. The bones of Lycidas, wherever they may be hurled, are perhaps at the whim of Nature as being outside the charmed 'pastoral' world. But it could, alternatively, be said that that pastoral world is a pipe-dream and shown to be such in the course of Milton's poem; if that disappears, there is no distinction between Nature and 'pastoral'. It could equally be maintained that the land of the Scholar-Gipsy is not 'pastoral' but 'nature', since it is based on detailed description of scenery which we know to have existed. But that 'nature' also is a walled garden of the imagination, in contrast to the more spacious and problematic world outside. *In Memoriam* has no consistent 'pastoral' or 'natural' setting, but it has a faith or a progressive outlook which it tries to preserve against a panoramic background of Nature's indifference, exemplified by the death of Hallam and what the evolutionists had declared as the cycle of cataclysms revealed by geology.

In short, however we look at it, we find a world of the imagination under assault by powerful forces from outside. The seasons, the sap, the stars – these are sometimes in the one world and sometimes outside it, but always they are closely connected with the theme. There are degrees of artifice, certainly, and we cannot ignore them. It is convenient to term the classically-derived shepherdry 'pastoral' and the native countryside 'nature'. It is also convenient to refer to that which appears elemental as 'Nature'. But really there is a continuity between 'nature' and 'pastoral' and they are not taken to be either exclusive or self-dependent; they evidence alike the possible character of the power which governs all things.

The Mourner and the Mourned

Personal elegy is essentially a lamentation for an individual, whose attributes one might expect to be sung at some length. But, in the first place, whilst it might be argued that those who mourned the death of Adonis were in fact using him as a representation of some personal loss, it seems certain that he was primarily an idea, a fertility god whose death was bewailed in an annual ritual – as Bion's *Lament for Adonis* concludes,

> *Cease, Cytherea, from thy lamentations, today refrain from thy dirges. Thou must again bewail him, again must weep for him another year.*[12]

In the second place, even (perhaps especially) in the fertility ritual, the lament and tribute were inseparable from therapeutic benefits to those

9

who offered them, whether to the singers in the poem, or to the poet[13] or to both. If it was essential that the departed be seen to achieve the reward of their merits, the recognition of their powers, either through annual celebration to an influence believed to be still existing, or in an afterlife of eternal bliss, it was also by doing justice to the dead, even propitiating them, that the mourners achieved a readjustment to everyday life.

In the early elegies the tribute was frequently the building of a tomb. Thus the shepherds in Virgil's *Eclogue V* are to build a tomb with epitaph and to lay on annual rites. In Bryskett's *Pastoral Eclogue on the Death of Sir Philip Sidney* (1595), flowers are strewn on the bier, nymphs are to deck the tomb and shepherds to render yearly praises. In the Renaissance elegy *Alcon* of Castiglione, where Alcon dies far from home, the bereaved Iolas builds and has decked with flowers an empty tomb, when his friend Leucippus, who was with Alcon on the fatal day, has already done the honours abroad. But, and especially later, the ultimate memorial is the singing of the song, the making of the poem itself. The shedding of the 'melodious tear', as it is put in *Lycidas*, is akin to the annual rites and the building of the tomb, and plainly this is a main means of adjustment. This concentration upon the work of art and its effect on the poet (and reader) had been developed greatly beyond the seeds which are present in classical elegies, until in *In Memoriam*, perhaps the climax of the tradition, the charting of the poet's changing state of mind (or that of the persona within the poem) as he attempts to find consolation for his loss is the principal subject of the work, which becomes more by inference than defined statement a celebration of the dead Hallam:

> *I leave thy praises unexpressed*
> *In verse that brings myself relief,*
> *And by the measure of my grief*
> *I leave thy greatness to be guessed.* (lxxv)

Thyrsis and *Adonais* are concerned with the early deaths not only of kindred spirits but with the deaths of poets. The circumstances of Gray's *Elegy* which apply to the poem we cannot for certain determine, but we do know that Edward King, the subject of *Lycidas*, held a Cambridge fellowship whilst preparing for the ministry and wrote verse in a small way. Arthur Hallam, whilst Tennyson and others viewed his future role as that of a statesman ('A life in civil action warm, A soul on highest mission sent, A potent voice of Parliament' – cxiii), was a poet and writer of some promise (Tennyson incorporates fragments of his poetry into *In Memoriam*). One of the most celebrated classical elegies is for the poet Bion who had himself written the *Lament for Adonis*. Virgil's *Eclogue V* concerns Daphnis as the divine type of the pastoral poet (the poet, that is, with a vital function towards his people). It is no accident that Milton brings into *Lycidas* the archetypal poet-minstrel, Orpheus. The death of the poet cannot but bring to mind the poetic purpose and the future death of that other poet who is now writing. Thus 'Milton' (that is, perhaps, the 'swain' spokesman) contemplates a similar memorial –

> *So may some gentle Muse*
> *With lucky words favour my destin'd Urn –*
>
> (*Lycidas* 19–20)

and Shelley is one 'who in another's fate now wept his own' (*Adonais* 300). Again, according to one's reading of the poem, it may well be that Gray or his speaker, hitherto 'mindful of the unhonoured dead', proceeds to envisage for himself a suitably reticent 'Epitaph'. From the turning of the attention of the mourner from the person he has loved to his own abandoned and possible future state stems the custom in these poems to scrutinise the whole nature and value of poetic art in general and as it is, or will be, practised by the spokesman himself. If it may be a study of amatory or political problems in a sort of laboratory, a 'little academe', isolated from irrelevant aspects of reality, pastoral is also frequently a study of poetic art and its purpose.

The dual role of elegy, as memorial and self-expression, is crucial, and it is of particlar importance in the lament by a poet for a poet. As a memorial, the work may itself be felt to have power to defeat time, to bestow a sort of immortality comparable to the 'Fame' of which the dead poet has been deprived by his early demise. This is the theme of 'Your monument shall be my verse' and 'so long lives this, and this gives life to thee' familiar from Shakespeare's Sonnets (Nos. 81 and 18). It seems as if the flowers strewn on a hearse or tomb in earlier days are in part replaced by the poem itself. So in King's *Exequy* we have

> *And for sweet flowers to crown thy hearse*
> *Receive a strew of weeping verse,*

and, in *In Memoriam*, the fantasy of

> *And this poor flower of poesy*
> *Which little cared for fades not yet,*
>
> *But since it pleased a vanished eye*
> *I go to plant it on his tomb.* (viii)

But if the poem succeeds in making this idea plausible (though it may well occur as a conventional topos and conceit rather than as representing the possibility of any very profound consolation), it will inevitably achieve also a similar immortality for the mourner. Granted that 'Fame' is not vaingloriously defined (and Milton in *Lycidas* makes a careful distinction,

11

as does Gray in his *Elegy*) then if the poet's art now and in future can be rightly directed, he may have found for himself the purpose, the vindication of 'that alone which knows', which had seemed to be cast into doubt by the indiscriminate hand of Fate in permitting the death of an individual, even of a poet, whose (as he claims) manifest potential was unfulfilled. It is not merely that the lines may be read when he is gone, though that on a lower level is consolation, but that he is able to prove in the creation of the elegy that poetic art can supremely celebrate what he believes to be timeless. Its nature, being in its own way timeless (and one element of its timelessness is a paradoxical removal from the personal to the impersonal), symbolises the spirit which survives death.

Or so it may seem to the poet of Christian tradition writing for a Christian audience. To the pre-Christian poet or the poet of the Age of Doubt, the thing is less clear-cut. He may, with the writer of the *Lament for Bion*, still suggest the influence of poetry and music on the Gods, an influence whose contingency (on what, we hardly know) and fragility is embodied in the story of Orpheus and Eurydice. He may estimate what role his own poetry could play in such an intercession:

> But ah, if I might have gone down like Orpheus to Tartarus or as once Odysseus or Alcides of yore, I too would speedily have come to the house of Pluteus, that thee perchance I might behold, and if thou singest to Pluteus, that I might hear what is thy song ... But if I, even I, and my piping had aught availed, before Pluteus I too would have sung.[14]

The ritual and therapeutic aspects of expression he is almost bound to stress:

> And my Melpomene replies,
> A touch of shame upon her cheek,
> 'I am not worthy even to speak
> Of thy prevailing mysteries;
>
> For I am but an earthly Muse,
> And owning but a little art
> To lull with song an aching heart,
> And render human love his dues...
>
> I murmured, as I came along,
> Of comfort clasped in truth revealed...
>
> (*In Memoriam* xxxvii)

But, whatever form his appeal takes, he will still attempt to assess the worth of the dead poet and of his own poetic purpose by reference to some

12

external transcedent symbol or value which he and the departed might have had in common. Thus, in *Thyrsis* – although it will be no use imitating the past, when 'some good survivor' would cross the Styx 'piping a ditty sad for Bion's fate' to Pluto's wife Proserpina, since, though she was well acquainted with pastoral Sicily, 'of our poor Thames she never heard' – there can be found an 'omen', in the favourite tree (so important in this tradition) and its associations with what Arnold and Clough had made of the Scholar-Gipsy, that the values to which they were dedicated still live on.

Patterns of Consolation

With a large emphasis on the power of poetic art itself, the elegy moves towards acceptance and adjustment, but an acceptance and adjustment possible only because they appear to incorporate the essence of that which, in physical terms, is dead. It is because the acceptance brought by the mere passage of time seems inevitably to involve the lessening of grief with the lessening of love, the belittling and even forgetting of that which was most esteemed, that the consolation of passing years (the 'he'll get over it' syndrome) is refused; it would be a submission to that which has already won the first round, it would cast doubt on the assertion that 'love is more than in the summers that are flown'.

The classical elegy does not make much of consolation or the search for consolation. There is some element of the theme, with immortality conceived as cyclic life, in the annual ritual, which may have been more important to this poetry in earlier stages than surviving references suggest. But, though Orpheus gains entry to Hades and song prevails, it does so only so far, and it seems that the worlds of the living and the dead cannot be bridged. That the songs of Bion or his mourner might prevail over Persephone seems primarily a charming conceit which emphasises the finality of death (if also the power ascribed to song) rather than offering actual likelihood of comfort.[15] In this respect, Virgil's lament for Daphis (*Ecloque V*) goes far beyond that of his model, Theocritus (*Idyll 1*), where the poet beloved of the Muses died, apparently for refusing to love, a semi-Promethean figure firm to his ideal, whirled down the stream, unable to be saved by Aphrodite, and with no mention of a future life. By contrast, Virgil's Daphnis, supreme poet and lover on earth, identified with Orpheus and Apollo in his heavenly role (and conveniently made a fertility god in Pope's version, the *Winter* pastoral) is elevated to heaven and the stars and becomes the subject of annual worship. Whether or not this innovation was particularly a tribute on Virgil's part to Caesar is not to our present point. What is important rather is the double consolation, of annual celebration and apotheosis, in respect of the ideal shepherd-poet-lover, for that makes thoroughly explicit the duality of consolation which

13

extends right through the tradition, and pervades our poems from *Lycidas* to *In Memoriam*.

The immense concern with the value of poetry, the excellence of the dead shepherd's singing, the poet's or speaker's relationship to him in the league-table of sweetness and the efficacy of song to calm the flocks, are an association of the dead with the living in a common purpose. The poet going about his business represents order – but his immediate problem is to produce the order of art in his grief. So the composing of the memorial piece, the taking part in the ritual, is a continuation of that union which first appearances suggest to have been shattered. The self-expression is the consolation, the continuation of the dead man's past, though how far this represents live belief and how far it represents a convenient conceit, perhaps founded on earlier belief, it is idle to enquire. The experience of death, the transcendence through art, is an essential qualification of the poet, the test which he must pass before he can fulfil his life's artistic purpose. To Thyrsus, in Theocritus's poem, will be given, if he sing the lament for Daphnis sufficiently well, an enigmatic reward, a sort of badge, a wooden bowl, carved, within a border of acanthus leaf, with pastoral scenes – some sort of poetic programme, perhaps, but first and foremost a work of art mysterious as that 'leaf-fringed legend' of love set for all time on the Grecian Urn of Keats. For, in the great elegies, we are not in that 'realm of Flora and old Pan' which the Keats of *Sleep and Poetry* outgrew, even if it is of that that we first think in contemplating pastoral. We are rather in the preferred world of 'the agonies, the strife Of human hearts'.[16]

Subsequently, the two strands of consolation – the memorial and the apotheosis – which we find closely linked in *Lycidas*, become more separate and distinct. A consolation more fully developed, worked out within the poem rather than brought in, seems to be required, with a greater or more immediate assurance that there is stability beyond change. Aspects of the classical picture no longer apply. Where there has been the formula 'What could the nymphs have done?' (as in Theocritus, *Idyll I*, developed by Virgil *Eclogue X*, and in *Lycidas*) within the pastoral world, there comes the question 'What could intercession with Persephone do?' in the Thames countryside so remote from the Doric world of antiquity where there was a conveniently 'easy access to the hearer's grace' (*Thyrsis*, 91). Or the classical pastoral is a less certain part of the poem's total purpose (on the whole, for instance, it provides only the first half of *Adonais*). It is interwoven with passages of immediate questioning and doubt, its detail (the strewing of flowers on the tomb or hearse, the ritual consolation) applicable only as a 'false surmise', a form of expression not suitable to the circumstances of death in *Lycidas*. The memorial aspect of consolation is present in *Lycidas*, but not greatly developed. The uncouth swain who at the end of the day twitches his mantle blue and wonders about tomorrow's programme is evidently in a different state from him who at the outset felt compelled unseasonably to pluck the berries, and it appears that this change has been produced by the enforced utterance which constitutes the poem between beginning and end, but this therapy does not receive comment. In *In Memoriam*, by contrast, the progress of the mourner is assessed and his steps towards consolation and adjustment are constantly reviewed. *Adonais* reveals itself to have been concerned as much with the poet's orientation to the immortal and essential One as with any personal bereavement. As in Keats, so in Arnold and Tennyson, the 'realm of Flora and old Pan' is a world to which allusion is made, distinct from the whole matter of the poetry; but, it may be felt, the whole 'natural' context of these later elegies is itself based on conventional views of reality, limited and repeated settings which are an extension of the old pastoral world, and no less a simplification with a profound purpose. Arnold, Thyrsis and the Cumnor Countryside with regard to the modern city are as Theocritus and Doric Sicily with regard to the society of Alexandria, but to Arnold the relationship is problematic and in part the subject of his poem.

Concepts of Form

The increased self-consciousness, the increasing awareness of themes which were always latent, the inclination to centre more upon the state of mind of the mourner, and, of course, the associated tendency to write about writing, lead to a change of form. We can perhaps indicate it by starting from the assumption that elegy is basically a dramatic form; someone (normally a shepherd or goatherd) is depicted making a memorial speech or uttering a lament for someone else. He is often alone, so that the whole performance appears to be overheard. From the outset there are open to the poet the possibilities of developing the singer or his subject or both equally. In Theocritus's *Idyll I*, perhaps the archetype of pastoral elegies, a substantial part of the poem is a complaint by the dying Daphnis, set within the framework of Thyrsis's lament for Daphnis dead. But whatever the emphasis it is essential to the form that the speaker is in some degree an imagined being within the work of art rather than the poet himself. This has to be borne in mind with late elegies particularly, where the speaker may not be very distinctly portrayed or characterised and we refer, on the whole legitimately, but not always with due care, to 'Shelley' or 'Tennyson' when we mean the first-person narrator or speaker.

In the classical elegy, in part no doubt because of our ignorance but surely also because of the prevailing conceptions of art, the problem of the poet does not loom large. We cannot know whether Bion in his *Lament for Adonis* was representing under Adonis some lost friend or beloved and himself in the guise of Aphrodite. Perhaps the point is that, although this is improbable in view of the poem's reference to annual ritual and the sensuous presentation of the love between Venus and Adonis within the poem, it would hardly be possible to exclude one's own experiences, real and imagined, from such a piece. The whole question of the primitiveness or sophistication, the individuality or collectiveness, of early pastoral remains under debate. Yet, although it must of necessity contain a personal element, Bion's poem appears to present a dramatic situation of death and mourning which is complete in itself and not dependent on detailed external reference; it has the appearance of being an object rounded and self-contained, and it would still have that appearance if it were at some time found to be an elaborate cryptogram. The same may be said of the *Lament for Bion* (where, however, the mourner is the poet's persona and the extant poem is incomplete), and of Virgil's *Eclogues*, filled as they are with allusions, some of which doubtless remain to be discovered; they present dramatised situations where, if the poet appears, it is as a part of the poems' worlds not as a visitor whose concerns are constrasted with those worlds.[17] In English, Spenser preserves this dramatic conception in *The Shepheardes Calendar*. The elaborate device of the interpretative 'gloss', whatever part Spenser himself may have played in producing it, serves to distance the poet from the poems, even as he is present in the pastoral guise of Colin. The 'dialect', a device employed by many pastoral writers to suggest what they took to be the primitiveness and rusticality of pastoral, has a similar effect. The contemporary references, notably to the Church, are made in an allegorical fashion which absorbs them into the pastoral framework.[18]

Lycidas, whilst it still contrives to relate everything to an extended and partly Anglicized pastoral world like Spenser's, presents a departure by reason of the variety of styles it employs and to which it draws our attention. Its licence is not perhaps greater than that of its Renaissance predecessors, but Milton, no doubt because of his deeply classical background, is conscious of the difficulty of finding the right overall level of style (of resolving, perhaps, the manners of Theocritus and Virgil) and, more particularly, is conscious of style itself in a dramatic way, of the interrelations of the sections of his poem almost as if they were characters in a play. Broadly, classical pastoral predominates in the parts directly concerned with King, and a 'higher mood' and 'dread voice' in the so-called digressions where the personal implications prompted by King's death are explored. The whole is nonetheless within a pastoral frame (partly because Milton uses the by then established ambiguity of the word 'pastor' as a bridge to ecclesiastical concerns) and the same is true of the concluding section on the 'uncouth swain'. Yet the swain strikes the reader with a calculated shock, even though the return to the mourner after an apotheosis was conventional. We have been prepared for a contrast between pastoral and present reality (in part perhaps the object of the angel's 'ruth') and we expect to return from the marriage in heaven either to that reality or to the country of the mind to which the false surmise of the flowers and the hypothetical resting-places of Lycidas's body have accustomed us. Instead, we are faced with what must be, in relation to those, the artificial world of the hoary swain; and this, it seems, was the dramatic setting of the whole poem – the departures from and returns to Doric minstrelsy were aspects of the swain's grief, the near-violations of decorum were no accidents but calculated presentations of distress. The inadequacy of a single accepted style points to grief. Thus the poem, whilst it hardly breaks with the dramatic conception of elegy (whilst indeed it triumphantly asserts it), extends the boundaries very considerably; that sensuously depicted country of the mind, and that speaker uncertainly detached from the poet, become important features of later elegies, ousting the simpler and more self-contained classical tradition.

The monody of alternate doubts and assurances, griefs and consolations, parallels the numerous earlier elegies (of which Virgil's *Eclogue V* is the classic example) in dialogue form, where one voice provides the lamentation and another provides the consolation. But it is clear that the monody, of which *Lycidas* is in English perhaps the greatest and certainly the most influential example, lends itself to reflections which are neither wholly fictional nor wholly autobiographical, for the speaker of a monody is hardly constrained by a specific audience. The poet may not conceive of himself as a swain of any sort, let alone place himself within the poem as a distinct personage described by himself or others. In short, the monody provides the ideal battle-ground for exponents of the 'biographical heresy'[19]. It is the habit of the Nineteenth Century poet to use the pronouns 'I' and 'thou', where 'I' may or may not be more or less identified with himself, and 'thou' may or may not be the 'dear reader' of the corresponding formula in prose. This is of course a rather different problem from that in Gray's *Elegy*, where 'thee' refers to a character in the poem, whoever that character may be, and the first person does not appear, save in the fourth line. We are concerned rather with whether the loss experienced by the mourner is significantly a loss known to have been experienced by the poet, and whether the consolation which the mourner finds is offered to us by direct communication, as in a sermon, or as part of a poem (which might include precept of some sort), a more complex matter altogether.

This is a fundamental issue. Although it may be agreed that no character in a poem can fully represent the poet, there is of course a certain convenience and limited truth in referring to the words of Milton's uncouth swain as the words of the poet – 'Milton considers contemporary

17

threats to the true Church', and so forth. By that, we do not mean that they are a direct communication, almost regardless of the medium, from us to him. Plainly, if they were, their nature would not have been so debated. It is manifestly impossible for a character in a poem actually to *be* his creator, for a poet can only be a condensation, a brief abstract of the life to which it relates. It is scarcely possible actually to confuse character and author. The temptation is rather to assume that, because the outlook of the one appears to be consistent with the outlook of the other, the character must be a mouthpiece for the poet's point of view (and then to add to the character attributes which are not in and may actually conflict with the poem). The temptation is of course all the stronger if the character has a persuasive role or, as a mourner, would appear to attract identification as a human being lost (as who is not lost in the contemplation of death?) in the endeavour to make sense and justice of the human predicament. To draw from the utterances of the character inferences as to the poet's beliefs can scarcely be justified. To draw from our knowledge of the poet's belief inferences about the behaviour of the character is rather to imply that the character is not fully realised and self-sufficient within the created work; the data of history and biography do not (or did not) survive time as does the rounded work of art, and to invoke the one to interpret the other is ultimately to limit rather than to enlarge the relevance of the poem.

These are, despite some difficulties, tenable distinctions when we are confronted with such as the uncouth swain at beginning and end, when the speaker exists in a setting other than that described by himself. They become less so when, as in *In Memoriam*, the predominant pronoun is the first person and we are presented with a time-scheme which, if it does not match at every point the circumstances of Tennyson's loss, points in its particularity to events which cannot be fully set out in the poem and therefore must be presumed to refer to life outside it (as, for example, the 'four sweet years' and 'fifth autumnal slope' of *In Memoriam* xxii). It is then not easy, it is perhaps not entirely natural, to regard the poem as entirely a dramatised realisation of the course of a grief. And what, in this context, are we to make of *Adonais*, where in the first part, which follows many of the conventions of formalised pastoral elegy, the speaker introduces himself as 'I', joins himself with others (presumably the reader, for he has no consistent audience in the poem) to see life as a perplexing play ('Of what scene The actors or spectators?' – 184–5) and then refers to the poet, his creator, in the third person, as a 'frail form, A phantom among men' (271ff), as one of the traditional procession of mourners who 'in another's fate now wept his own'? Have we actor, spectator and poet, rolled into one? It can be discovered who in the complex texture of *Adonais* is speaking at a particular time, but it does not strike one spontaneously (perhaps it does not need to), and by the time of the conclusion the 'I' whose bark is driven towards the One is far from distinctly the 'I' who began or the 'herd-abandoned deer' who mourned. We have not a clearly rendered spokesman and the opportunity to develop one, presented by the mourner in the procession, is not taken. The poet, as nearly as may be, addresses us direct.

Arnold specialises in the unclear spokesman. In *The Scholar-Gipsy*, the speaker finds himself a 'nook' o'er the half-reaped field' (21) and settles down to read Glanvill's account of the Scholar. After giving the gist of this, he suddenly addresses the Scholar-Gipsy direct ('And I myself seem half to know thy looks' – 62), as he does for the rest of the poem, not returning to the nook with its poppies and corn, and not (although he has told the shepherd he will be there 'till sundown') resorting to the classical pattern of dusk with the real prospect of another day, but fleeing into the huge and enigmatic simile of the Tyrian trader, ending, it seems, in a world of pure art. Meanwhile, he has identified himself with 'us' of modern civilisation, opposed, unless saved by some revelation of the Gipsy's spirit, to acceptable values. The poem forgets the dramatic setting with which it started and ends with a total immersion in the relationship which the 'poet' seems to be putting over, and the pastness of the pastoral or 'natural' scenes described, a part of its theme, makes it elegiac in general rather than personal terms. By contrast, *Thyrsis* is declared to be a 'monody' and scrupulously maintains that form until the end where the speaker, in one interpretation, turns to address himself as 'thou'. It is a speech not by a shepherd but by one who is now (lamentably) a confessed stranger to the pastoral or 'natural' world. It also offers an interpretation of its precipitating background (the career and death of Arthur Hugh Clough) which is at variance with known biographical fact, and it is a question whether this version is sufficiently plausible or consistent within itself for the poem to stand on its own. Close as it might formally appear to the classical monody, the poem illustrates how very far we have come from classical pastoral. It is not that there is personal expression, albeit through the mouth of a visitor to the country, of a sense of division between the pastoral and real worlds. Such expression is itself a convention. Virgil, struck by some irrelevance of pastoral to the true concerns of his day, appears in his *Eclogue IX* to contemplate writing a national epic. Milton, in his *Epitaphium Damonis* (as also perhaps in the 'pastures new' of *Lycidas*) considers hanging up the pastoral pipes and working on an Arthurian project in the vernacular. Spenser and Keats in moving from pastoral to epic were following the classical pattern recommended by countless Renaissance and later pundits. But in *Thyrsis* the 'rustic' flute moved on to the world 'of men contention-tossed, of men who groan', only to be abandoned, a silence which seems to threaten the speaker also. It is not that the pastoral is abandoned, but that the real world itself has for the mourner been abandoned in search of whatever verities may remain embodied in the world of the Scholar-Gipsy. That world is opposed to the 'city noise' in which the poet's life is spent, and it is proposed that it offer a 'whisper' of consolation in this unsympathetic and otherwise largely valueless reality. We cannot say it is an anti-pastoral treatment, for clearly these are themes frequently suggested by and sometimes explicit in pastoral. What is disconcerting is the *openness* of the admission (so much of attitudes, of the relating of pastoral to reality, is commonly implied), and the enormous (one senses, too enormous) burden of responsibility placed on 'nature'; this is asking more of pastoral than its dramatic form will bear, and it is perhaps also asking more than 'nature' can give. We sense impossibility, and elegy in the general sense, in the tone; ostensibly the mourning is for one who 'of his own free will' left the pastoral world, but we feel an element of self-pity for the mourner who needs must 'into the world and wave of men depart'.

The explicit relating of worlds felt to be opposed puts a strain on conventional forms, and it can hardly be directed anywhere but at the reader. Therefore, although technically a monody, *Thyrsis* seems to share with the other elegies after Gray an extreme uncertainty as to its formal boundaries; its mode of address to the reader is more direct than it would appear to be and it is not the complete and reflecting artefact that its classical profile leads us to expect. If we accept that, which implies a gradual change in the nature of poetry, the question of whether the speaker is the poet *in propria persona*, or a surrogate within the poem who to an uncertain degree represents the poet, is perhaps academic. It might be expected that a poet in the age of Browning (who according to Arnold was 'a man with a moderate gift passionately desiring movement and fullness, and containing but a confused multitudinousness'[20]) who proposed to write a 'monody' would be impelled to produce some form of 'dramatic monologue', and the interpretative problem would then have been considerable. But *Thyrsis* is very far from such a thing and its speaker is never seen, nor ever sees himself, from the outside. He is no more or less a monodist than the first person of Keat's *Ode to a Nightingale* – to which *Thyrsis* and *The Scholar-Gipsy* are considerably indebted.

As we shall see, the speaker of *In Memoriam* puts us into a similar quandary. It is possible that in the Victorian Age there was a certain urgency or solemnity about elegy by which, though its individual and private nature was stressed, it became part of a sense of public duty, at a time when the nature of public duties was in debate. Perhaps the sense of loss (not merely personal loss), and the need in the face of scientific controversy to find unshifting consolation, led to a lessening of the dramatic and fictive element and a heightening of the expressive. The ideal of the expressive monument is not abandoned, but it comes under pressure.

We have seen how at the heart of elegy is a duality. The very process of ordering grief, whether real or imaginary, into a work of art may be the consolation the search for which is the ostensible subject of the poem. The finding of form coincides with the defeat of grief and the finished work is in some sense a triumph over Time. The image of flowers of poesie is not these days a very appealing one. And yet we can be so solemn in our search for profundities of content that we take insufficient note of the profundity of an artistic whole, such as no doubt is suggested by the carved bowl of Theocritus's *Idyll*. Even the word 'monument' brings to mind the 'storied urn or animated bust' rather than the 'uncouth rhymes and shapeless sculpture' which, in Gray's contention, may be no less monumental. I do not say that we can be satisfied with what is finally uncouth and shapeless. They are not art. Yet a monument is in origin merely something which reminds, a memorial, not necessarily an unwieldy statue. It is essentially an object, a unity, and it is the paradox of art, and the core of personal elegy, that a sequence of communicating words, produced by self-expression and able to influence the reader by example, may become a monument, a symbol which, though it is read as a sequence, is nevertheless more than a sequence.

Thus the elegy which arrives at a consolation does not leave us with consolation and say that the problem is solved. It presents us with the quest, inseparable from its ending in the work of art. The building of the tomb, whether occupied or empty, and the decking with flowers, whether real or of 'poesie', represent the producing of the expressive monument in words, and it is particularly with this duality of expression and the making of the object, inherent in this tradition, that these studies are concerned.

II

Milton – *Lycidas*

There is, I think, interesting common ground beneath the views of Johnson and Auden on *Lycidas*. Johnson, it will be remembered, objected in his *Life of Milton* that 'It is not to be considered as the effusion of real passion; for passion runs not after remote allusions and obscure opinions ... Where there is leisure for fiction there is little grief. In this poem there is no nature, for there is no truth; there is no art, for there is nothing new. Its form is that of a pastoral, easy, vulgar, and therefore disgusting.' Auden's opinion is that 'At first reading, *Lycidas* seems to be by Prospero, for it purports to deal with the most serious matters possible – death, grief, sin, resurrection. But I believe this to be an illusion. On closer inspection it seems to me that only the robes are Prospero's and that Ariel has dressed up in them for fun ... If *Lycidas* is read in this way, as if it were a poem by Edward Lear, then it seems to me one of the most beautiful poems in the English language...'[1]

What these views have in common (and Auden goes on to endorse Johnson's criticism except that he believes Johnson could have mistaken Milton's aim) relates most obviously to the artificiality of the poem, but also, perhaps more essentially, to some question of gravity and basic sincerity. Johnson assumes (perhaps a little unfairly in view of the known convention) that elegy should express in a convincing manner profound and personal grief, and such grief he does not find. Auden does not find it either, and he proposes (again, perhaps a little unfairly, and with a perceptible wink) that therefore it was never meant to be there (though whether he means Milton 'sent up' the tradition or that it has itself been misread over the centuries is unclear).

Johnson and Auden criticise the poem in the light of expressive content as it might be expected to strike the reader. Rightly or wrongly, the reader is not impressed with the feeling that Milton or the speaker has been moved by grief and, as a result, produced this poem. (For the moment we will leave aside the assumption that poet and speaker are or ought to be identical.) It will be reasonable, I think, to maintain that Auden – who, after all, can see his way to admiring the thing on his own terms, and Johnson – who does not admire it on any – represent extremes, the one in the assertion of expression (and intention inferred), and the other in the assertion of the object, the monument (and intention ignored). As has been said, elegy, whilst it may swing to one or other polarity, essentially partakes of both, and we have to consider *Lycidas* in this light.

Of personal grief arising from personal loss, rather than an imagined grief for the idea of loss, that is not, certainly, much sign in *Lycidas*. It may be that we have small evidence of the form's being used to express such grief or it may be that the form disguised the grief but, either way, the absence is unremarkable. The difference from general precedent is our knowledge that the poem is concerned not with a notability but with one who could conceivably have inspired such feeling. On the other hand, Milton's prefatory note saying that King was 'a learned Friend' scarcely suggests a close connection. Edward King was a year behind Milton at Christ's College, Cambridge, and was awarded a fellowship in 1630, after which he continued to prepare himself for the ministry, and had a tutorial role at the College, until his drowning in 1637 whilst on a visit to Ireland to see friends and relations. The ship struck a rock not far from the British coast, and King went down saying his prayers (according to the note in the commemorative volume *Justa Edovardo King* (1638), in the second part of which – *Obsequies to the Memorie of Mr Edward King* – *Lycidas* was first published as the final piece). That is appropriate but very likely hypothetical, as is the statement of Edward Phillips (Milton's nephew) that for King Milton 'had contracted a particular Friendship and Intimacy'.[2]

If the re-creation of time spent together, whether in pastoral fiction or in reality, is evidence of the depth of sensations of loss, then *Lycidas*, again, does not seem strongly motivated. Johnson says of the following lines that they are literally untrue, and allegorically 'uncertain and remote':

> *We drove a field, and both together heard*
> *What time the Gray-fly winds her sultry horn,*
> *Batt'ning our flocks with the fresh dews of night.*
>
> (27–9)

He contrasts them with Cowley's *On The Death of Mr William Hervey*, which is pastoral in the sense that it is fancifully 'natural' but, from Johnson's point of view, has the merit that it does not make a shepherd out of a student:

> *Ye fields of Cambridge, our dear Cambridge, say,*
> *Have ye not seen us walking every day?*

> *Was there a Tree about which did not know*
> *The Love betwixt us two?*
> *Henceforth, ye gentle Trees, for ever fade;*
> *Or your sad branches thicker joyn,*
> *And into darksome shades combine,*
> *Dark as the Grave wherein my friend is laid.*[3]

The invocation to the trees to mourn, to which *Lycidas* also refers, is not
'nature' or 'new', in Johnson's words, yet to this Johnson presumably does
not object – though he notes of the poem (in the *Life of Cowley*) that there
is 'little passion' and 'when he wishes to make us weep, he forgets to weep
himself'.

It is not mere whim which suggests to Milton that King and he be
represented as fellow-shepherds. There is, we may infer from the partly
conventional analysis of the Church in terms of a sheepfold, one reason in
the vocation of King; the pastor is the shepherd. There is another, of far
greater antiquity, not in blindly following precedent, but in the
interweaving of song, society and work in the Sicilian countryside as
described or recalled by Theocritus. Here is an association of pastoral with
the origins of poetry (practically rather than historically, it may be) and
with poetic purpose which is very much present in *Lycidas*. Indeed, it is
not so much the 'disguise' of King as shepherd, in itself, to which Johnson
seems to react, as the detail with which the analogy is developed (by way of
the 'Rural ditties' and tutor 'old Damoetas') without a clear reference –
though the name-dropping without explanation or introduction is very
characteristic of pastoral. We think that being nursed on the self-same hill,
having fed the same flock, and having sung before Damoetas mean rather
the spirit of what Cowley refers to, but we cannot tell:

> *To him my Muse made haste with every strain*
> *Whilst it was new, and warm yet from the Brain.*
> *He lov'd my worthless Rhimes, and like a Friend*
> *Would find out something to commend.*
> *Hence now, my Muse, thou canst not me delight;*
> *Be this my latest verse*
> *With which I now adorn his Herse,*
> *And this my Grief, without thy Help shall write.*[4]

It is not, certainly, powerful, but it tells us something of the nature of a
relationship now lost, and a relationship between individuals. Of this there
is virtually nothing in *Lycidas* (though there is more in the *Epitaphium
Damonis* (1640) concerning Charles Diodati, with whom Milton had a
longer-lasting and (it is believed) closer relationship than with Edward
King). It may be that the haunting (though generalised) sense of loss

24

which we find in this section of Milton's poem can embarrass not because it stirs no emotions and seems born of none, but because it is not possible in the poem to find what it refers to. A personal relationship is not described as between individuals, yet the feeling of one person for another is suggested:

> For we were nurst upon the self-same hill,
> Fed the same flock, by fountain, shade, and rill...
> But O the heavy change, now thou art gon,
> Now thou art gon, and never must return!

(23-4, 37-8)

It is not to disparage the poem to suggest that as an elegy for King it is a duty, a set-piece possibly commissioned for the memorial volume, and commissioned at a distance, for Milton had not been in Cambridge for five years and we have no reason to suppose he had had any recent acquaintance with King. The first fourteen lines seem to suggest that something like this was the case – although they can conveniently suggest also that death was the real commissioner and one has no choice over the time of grief. There is considerable emphasis on the necessity of the undertaking. The fingers which pluck the berries are 'forc'd', 'bitter constraint ... compels', and 'he must not flote upon his watry bear Unwept'. In writing 'Who would not sing for Lycidas?' Milton introduces the notion that King was a poet of note (which is hardly true) and which is an important part of the identification with him on which the poem is built.[5] He also refers to Virgil's *Eclogue X* where, again speaking of a poet (Gallus) Virgil uses a similar expression, 'neget quis carmina Gallo?' Virgil's poem is something of an affectionate skit on Gallus's love-poetry, as well as a tribute, and the fact perhaps may reinforce our idea of *Lycidas* as a self-conscious artefact as well as an expression of the idea of grief. Virgil has invoked the fountain Arethusa (as Milton will invoke her, and also Mincius, the river of Virgil's birthplace), and he starts by calling his piece the 'extremum laborem', the last task of the whole collection. Whilst it seems undeniable that the shattering (i.e. scattering) of the leaves before the mellowing year and the disturbing of the 'season due' relate to the premature death (aged 24) of King, they seem to refer also to the invariable unseasonableness of grief and the imposition of writing an obituary (rather than the pressing and intimate necessity to express one's grief). The reluctance is itself conventional, a self-disparagement like the custom of being unaccustomed to public speaking, but not *merely* conventional, and so – 'Hence with denial vain and coy excuse', or 'Begin, then...', suggesting partly that the sooner it's started the sooner it will be ended. *Lycidas*, in this opening, is in some measure a poem of wit, and it may not be unreasonable to view its juggling with pastoral veins throughout as having that element in it.

After the opening oblique discussion of poetry and grounds for identification with King in the lines 'he well knew Himself to sing, and build the lofty rhyme', there comes what is superficially an idle fancy, but one on which it could be said that some of the key issues of the poem are grounded. For here is embodied the idea of elegy as memorial and the creator observing himself creating – the self-conscious artist – and here is heightened in the mind the identification of the speaker and King:

> So may some gentle Muse
> With lucky words favour my destin'd Urn,
> And as he passes turn
> And bid fair peace be to my sable shrowd

(19–22)

There is, again, wit in the idea, a continuation of the view of the poem as a 'favour' or duty; but also a genuine turning of the interest nearer to the mourner. 'So may' implies 'in the same way as I have announced', or 'as I am going to for him'. 'May', like the 'lucky' (good-omened) words and 'destin'd urn', conveys the idea of fate and also of influencing fate. It is partly modal in force; a similar elegy is not only a possibility (as against the certainty of death), but is actually wanted, and presumably to earn it the poet will have to equal the poetical powers he has, for the poem, attributed to King.

According to one textual reading here, the introductory paragraph then ends with the following lines ('For we were nurst upon the self-same hill...'), which become an argument in support of the speaker's having the same sort of elegy as King – they are, in effect, equals. In the other version, 'we were nurst...' begins the paragraph relating to pastoral kinship, and the introduction ends with 'my sable shrowd'. But, either way, the poem has turned strongly towards the likeness of the speaker and Lycidas, and the fact that Lycidas is dead has brought to the speaker the prospect of his own death, which will lead him in the poem to question his life's purpose.

The theme of unseasonableness in the opening, an unseasonableness there brought about by the poet's acting under the duress of the 'sad occasion dear', is taken up in the lament of Nature for the 'Shepherd', and it is notable that Lycidas's song is still in mind. It is the 'shepherd' himself that the woods and the caves mourn, but the willows and hazels will no longer fan their leaves to his 'soft layes'. By simile the 'loss to shepheards ear' (particularly, that is, the loss of the shepherd-singer) is compared to the canker in the rose and a late frost on flowers; the use of simile rather than metaphor is notable, for it keeps the tone down – Milton avoids the

26

more extreme imagery of Nature's lamenting which is so common throughout the tradition. But there is no comparison between Nature (the seasons) and the speaker's state of mind, and this may again suggest a lack of precipitating grief.

With the background, as it were – the poet's duty, his kinship with the dead man, the effect of the loss in general terms – now complete, the speaker turns to the circumstances of death which, considered in their horror (largely projected onto Orpheus), prompt probings as to the purpose of a life which can be so suddenly and with apparently so little justice terminated. Thinking again of the 'Gallus' *Eclogue* (X) of Virgil, where the speaker asks where were the saving Naiads (for they were not on Parnassus or Aganippe's fountain – both sacred to the Muses – at the time), and no doubt also of Virgil's source (Theocritus, *Idyll I* (67), where the nymphs were similarly not with Daphnis), Milton asks where the nymphs were when 'your lov'd Lycidas' was drowned, for they were not

> *Where your old Bards, the famous Druids ly,*
> *Nor on the shaggy top of Mona high* ... (54–5)

– that is, they were not in North Wales in a position, as muses should be, to save their poet. There enters then what is to become a characteristic of the poem (as of the later tradition), that is to say, a questioning of the convention which he has nonetheless set out. It is here, of course, that we become aware of the dramatic aspect of the monody; the speaker introduces possible solutions only to find them unacceptable. He is, as it were, overheard in his vacillation, but the overall movement towards assurance by eliminating the misconceptions obliges us to consider the poet as in control and as distinct from the speaker (as indeed does the beauty of what is rejected). The poem, moreover, following certain hints already given, is turning towards the spokesman, the mourner, as its subject – the identification is having its effect.

> *Ay me, I fondly dream!*
> *Had ye bin there ... for what could that have don?*

As the speaker thinks, 'after all, had the nymphs been in their proper places in Anglesey, what difference would that have made?', or, as the poet perhaps thinks, 'can there be any consolation within this pastoral mode for what has broken in from outside and upset the order to such an extent that the trees have lost their seasons?' – the speaker moves into an image of almost boundless implication. Orpheus, lamented by 'Universal nature', as Lycidas has been mourned by 'the Woods, and desert caves ... And all their echoes', his 'goary visage' cast 'down the swift Hebrus' by the Bacchantes in jealousy of his faithfulness to his dead wife Eurydice (a rather more common aspect of the myth in pastoral), seems in some degree to be Lycidas. The *Lament for Bion* indeed identifies Bion, the lamented poet, as 'the Dorian Orpheus'. At the least, Orpheus seems to have been called to mind by the fact that Lycidas had a watery end and, for the purposes of the poem, was a poet of distinction. If Orpheus could not be saved by his mother, the Muse Calliope, could Lycidas have been saved by his Nymphs or, for the echo may be there, by the intercession of the present Orpheus/poet?[6]

Having been led to consider the implications of this death as possibly outside the local pastoral world, the speaker enters on the first 'digression'. It is, of course, more a change of emphasis; Lycidas and the speaker are in several respects now identified, and he moves out at a tangent from this communion of spirit, which acts as a sort of meeting place, a point to return to, during the poem's apparent wanderings. Orpheus, who could not be saved by Calliope, who could not recall Eurydice in a lasting fashion, is the type of the dedicated poet-priest. What is considered is the poetry that is 'thankless' because it receives no obvious reward or recognition (we reflect back to the 'meed of some melodious tear' for Lycidas, of which this discussion is itself a part) and produces no obvious results. The speaker and the poet are here very close, for this is virtually a discussion of the merits of pastoral within a 'pastoral' context. The shepherd talking of a shepherd has gone, but Amaryllis, Neaera and Phoebus are not unknown in pastoral, and 'guerdon' and 'meed' (again) have an archaic and romantic flavour.

The discussion is closely involved with the fate of Lycidas, 'dead ere his prime' and therefore unfulfilled as poet or priest. 'Fame', the recognition of fulfilment, is seen as a prime motivating force in life and, superficially, it is most easily got in activities whose merits are most readily recognisable, pleasures such as sporting with Amaryllis in the shade. Fame, which cannot be assessed until life is complete, is thus at first conceived romantically, popularly, as the 'fair guerdon' of acclaim, a 'sudden blaze' corresponding, presumably, in most cases to a genuine value (for, whilst Milton contrasts the outward and the inner he does not regard them as inevitably incompatible here). In the simplest terms, this is the wish to be thought well of; it may be connected with personal grief (the universal wish to be remembered, as in Gray's *Elegy*) such as in *Lycidas* is little represented. And it is subject to Atropos, Fate, who has the aspect of a 'blind Fury'; it is limited by the eventual deaths of the attainer and of those who recognise him.

The 'praise' with which this aspect of Fame is contrasted is the recognition of true merit by Jove. It is not dependent on the lives of the beholders or 'broad rumour', but really 'lives'. It is not, and presumably that which achieves it is not, a matter of external appeal ('the glistering foil

Set off to th'world' suggests a jewel setting, which implies again that the same 'jewel' may receive both kinds of Fame and they not be mutually exclusive. We recall the unseen 'gem of purest ray serene' of Gray's *Elegy* (53)). This, it seems clear, is the Fame which the strictly meditated 'homely slighted Shepherds trade' may hope to win; sporting with Amaryllis in the shade is likely in itself to stop short at the 'glistering foil', to be a waste of true talent. And all this is the reply of Phoebus to the speaker, or Milton. It has its tangential relationship with Lycidas too early lost, but it refers more to the nexus of the two; it is for the benefit of the elegist and amounts to an assessment of the purpose of writing the elegy (it might uncharitably be suggested that Johnson associated *Lycidas* with Amaryllis rather than with the 'thankless Muse', but that Auden, by his response to the witty artifice and the tribute to poetry which it implies, avoided the confusion).

Reassured as to the purpose of serious poetry, the speaker returns to his purer pastoral, admitting that he has deviated from the strict convention by introducing the 'higher mood'[7] of his discourse with Apollo. But the 'higher mood' strangely lights the duteous diversion and it takes on a lyrical motion which will not allow us to contrast the one level absolutely with the other. The invocation of Arethusa and Mincius suggests a consciousness of having strayed from the guiding spirits of Theocritus and Virgil, and announces the return of his 'oat', to one of the most well-worn pictures of the convention – the procession of mourners. Triton (the 'Herald of the Sea') who comes at Neptune's request, has, however, a distinctive cast and he takes up the theme of the lament itself from the contemplation of death in the 'remorseless deep' where it was left (63). His purpose is to establish that man, rather than Nature, must be held responsible for the 'hard mishap (which) hath doom'd this gentle swain' (92). This suggestion – that 'It was that fatall and perfidious Bark' that was responsible[8] – may be in conflict with the Latin prefatory note to the volume, which does not mention the weather when the ship struck the rock, and it exonerates Nature by what seems something of a quibble (though the death remains equally incomprehensible). But its point is perhaps rather to stress the weight which Milton throughout gives to human conceptions and values. Thus there is irony here in the disruption by human agency of the natural order in which Panope and her sisters – believed favourable to sailors – were playing on the calm waters at the time. When all is said, it is, after all, a dilemma of the human predicament which cannot be resolved; the ship should have been built better, but the rock was there.

The River Cam appears, representing the place which Milton and Lycidas had in common, and apparently citing King as a special prodigy ('my dearest pledge'), wearing moreover a bonnet with a hyacinth-like design upon it (an almost obligatory allusion; Hyacinth

was loved by Apollo and so is peculiarly dear to pastoral elegists).
Then

> Last came, and last did go,
> The Pilot of the Galilean lake.

Phoebus was introduced in a tangential discussion of Fame prompted by
the theme of unfulfilled death. The St Peter episode, though the second
'digression', emerges directly from the conventional elegy, since St Peter
is the last of the procession of mourners. The Phoebus lines arose from the
hypothesis that Lycidas and the speaker might be identified as poets for
the space of the poem, a hypothesis which scarcely holds up outside it. But
King's dedication to the ministry and Milton's passionate interest in the
Church are far more closely linked and the speaker would in purpose
appear to be almost entirely subsumed into Milton himself during the
following passage.

The lines on St Peter are closely related to an earlier pastoral, Spenser's
May Eclogue, and the justification of both is in the Renaissance extension
of pastoral by way of the idea of Christ as the Good Shepherd, in which the
sheep in their fold are the Church and their shepherds are good or bad
ministers. An important seam in the imagery is concerned with greed for
the two objects of food and worldly wealth, and it is clear that the concern
with money and good living, at the expense of the flock, works against
values in both human and animal folds. The 'blind mouthes' who could
readily be dispensed with in favour of Lycidas, the exemplary priest of the
future, are condemned by the episcopal St Peter (though Milton would
later reject the role of bishops from his conception of the ideal church
system) because they 'creep and intrude, and climb into the fold', that is,
they enter the Church who do not belong to it, and they do so for purely
selfish motives ('for their bellies sake'). 'They are sped' – that is, '*they're* all
right' – and they proceed to issue bad food (teaching) or none, so that the
hungry sheep 'rot inwardly'. In all this they are contrasted with 'thee,
young swain', who is presumed to know 'the faithfull Herdsmans art'.
Meanwhile, a further intruder, the 'grim wolf with privy paw' also
'devours apace', eating the very sheep themselves, apparently sneaking
one here and there unnoticed ('privy'), but making substantial killings
('apace'). The usage of the comparison for at least a century indicates that
the 'wolf' represents Roman Catholicism. The others who creep and
intrude may well typify the followers of Laud, but at the least plainly
represent false clergy.

Spenser's *May Eclogue*, EK's gloss tells us, concerns 'the Pope and his
anti-Christian Prelates, which usurpe a tyrannical dominion of the
Churche, and with Peters counterfet keyes, open a wide gate to all
wickednesse and insolent government.' Spenser mentions a present

situation of hireling priests, with no care for their flock, compared with a preferred time when 'shepeheards had none inheritaunce, ne of land, nor fee in sufferance.' Complacency led to a search for 'greedie governaunce', 'lying soft' rather than 'living hard', and it was then that these Catholic wolves took advantage of the situation; secretly, 'full of fraud and guile', they 'crept in', operating like the 'privy paw'. They are, however, as in Milton, only part of the object of attack, which is primarily a seeking after worldly goods and high station, with which the Romans are associated in both poets' minds. The absentee prelate hires deputies 'that playen while their flocks be unfedde' – the lines 'But they bene hyred for little pay Of other, that caren as little as they What fallen the flocke' (47–9) seem to be recalled by Milton in 'Of other care they little reckning make' (116). Milton's 'shearers feast' may well owe something to the opening picture of this part of Spenser's poem, which is of a 'shole of shepheardes' processing home from a May Day ritual to the accompaniment of light music. Such, while the sheep are unfed or are in the charge of hirelings, pass their time 'In lustihede and wanton argument'. Their 'singing and shouting and jolly chere' (21) appear to be taken up in the 'lean and flashy songs' of Milton's 'blinde mouths', songs which, however, are directly related to the feeding of the sheep and so represent inadequate teaching. All this, in Spenser's account, will be assessed 'When great Pan account of shepeherdes shall aske' (54), where, in the gloss. 'Pan signifieth all or omnipotent, which is onely the Lord Jesus.' Milton's 'two-handed engine' is clearly the instrument by which similar 'account' will be taken[9], and, it has been suggested, possibly hearkens back to the 'abhorred shears' of Atropos (75) (though these are notable precisely for their indiscriminate action which is doubtfully appropriate of the 'engine').

It is unnecessary to labour the fact that this passage, part of the procession of mourners as it is, arises from the identification of Milton's own convictions with King's known dedication to a career in the Church, and that the equivocal meaning of 'pastoral' was the means of entry. What is perhaps less obvious, and more controversial, is the reference to the 'lean and flashy songs' of the uninvited guests, in particular their relevance to the theme of 'lofty rhyme' and 'thankles Muse' in the poem. It can hardly be doubted that they *are* related. Milton was ever aware of the theme of the poet-priest and was beginning to contemplate even now a poetic work which should be doctrinal to a nation – as the congregation are fed by the teaching of the priest, so the reading public (though 'few' may be 'fit' to benefit) are fed by the poet, and all, without disparagement, are akin to the sheep fed by the shepherd of whom Christ is the type. Moreover, the lean and flashy songs seem to echo the 'singing, shouting, and jolly chere' of the Spenserian revellers. But this good cheer, whilst the 'joysaunce' is condemned with regard to how the priests should be occupying themselves, nevertheless 'Made my heart after the pype to daunce' (*May*

31

Eclogue 26); there is in Spenser's poem, that is to say, an element of conflict between the pastoral delights and the ecclesiastical virtues (summarised in the Gloss's note which moves from Satan to Christ as the identity of Pan), which recalls that between Amaryllis and the true object of Fame. The 'lean and flashy songs' appear superficially to glance at the same conflict. But in Spenser's poem the equivalent diversion is a source of delight of a sort; it is that which conflicts with higher pastoral duties. In *Lycidas*, on the other hand, the songs in their very 'grating' sound (which is evidently more than an equivalent of the 'dry' sound attributed by Theocritus to the pipes) are rejected for their quality; they are not only entertainment at the wrong moment, but poor quality entertainment at that. Is there, then, an element of 'overkill' here, with Milton led, in the voice of Peter, into a double condemnation, in which good, thoroughly diverting songs would have been more convincing for the purpose? Is he, further, referring to a liturgy which he disliked? Are the songs poor stuff from the point of view of content, or technique, or both? 'When they list' means 'when they feel like it' (that is, rarely do they teach at all, and, when they do, they do it badly – this may recall Spenser's 'lustihede'), or 'when they (the sheep) listen' (Milton had used this archaic sense in *Comus* (480)). I think we can hardly settle for any one of these possibilities. What seems plain is the double image of religious and poetic teaching. The shepherd-priest is as the poet, offering poor food at his peril and awaiting some sort of 'account' by Jove, when Atropos has done her work, or by Christ when the 'two-handed engine' has struck. In this respect the 'Phoebus' and 'St Peter' passages are parallel, though if the 'two-handed engine' represents some cataclysmic reform of the church on earth there is evidently no parallel in respect of the pursuers of false Fame.

The is ample precedent for this type of thing in pastoral. Its presence in elegy as a part (rather than the making of a complete elegy into an allegory) is, however, another matter. Milton and his speaker are fictionally separated, the speaker within the poem being a 'real' shepherd, as is Lycidas, and St Peter being introduced as a sort of divinity in the traditional procession of mourners. But the extension into criticism of the contemporary church casts some doubt back onto this pastoral structure, for Lycidas and the clergy, whilst they are all shepherds by virtue of the concealed pun, are not alike shepherds of the particular hills on which the 'swain' is reflecting. Moreover, this passage presents a complaint of a different nature from the grief expressed by the swain. It is not so much that (as Johnson puts it) 'awful and sacred truths' are mingled with 'trifling fictions' or that the 'equivocations' are 'indecent, and at least approach to impiety', but that one untrifling fiction leads to another. Their connection can only exist in the mind of the speaker and of the speaker it has been designed that we think little until the end of the poem. But, whilst it differs from the introduction of Fame by virtue of the use of the 'mourner' in the procession, the passage on the Church does also importantly parallel that section in the fact that its point in relation to the pastoral is primarily that of tribute to Lycidas ánd the singing of the values which he is held to represent. St Peter – himself a *dramatis persona* created by the speaker who is created by Milton – could have 'spared' or done without the wolves and blind mouths 'for thee'. Lycidas was of the type to counteract the corruption – but he is dead. This church in chaos, the sheep dying of starvation, is the dim analogue of those many lamentable scenes in the convention where the grasses turn yellow and the leaves fall and the sheep starve for want of the dead shepherd. It is, as it were, an equal hyperbole, and it is possible to regard the speaker as responsible for it in his distressed state, rather than to assume that Milton was not in control of his fictions.

We are now becoming accustomed to the speaker's way. He acts plausibly as one grieved, having an outline and order in mind, departing on an urgent theme, and returning, and in this process creating a larger outline and order. The pastoral is as it were a compulsion, an assurance which breaks down, but to which he must nonetheless return. And so, ending his exploration of the tributary of the church, as he had ended his reflection on Fame, with the finality of Judgment in view, he returns to the 'stream' of his pastoral lament, adverting in passing to the changes of style involved (the first time, from a 'higher mood', and now from the 'dread voice' of St Peter). This is indicative of the ambiguous relation of the meditations to the mainstream, for the dread voice (unlike the passage on Fame arose directly from the convention and, whilst indeed the mood may be thought to receive some not wholly topical addition from the speaker and Milton, the pastoral setting has in a sense never been left, since St Peter utters his speech as he goes off-stage and we merely await the next happening. But the speaker seems to regard the two 'digressions' as equally tangential, since from the one he returns via Arethusa, and from the other via Alpheus,[10] lovers who became one and the same river. And, balancing the recall of Virgil through Mincius (86), he now invokes the 'Sicilian Muse' Theocritus (as had done Virgil in his *Eclogue IV* and as had done the *Lament for Bion*).

Yet, as soon as the speaker seems safely back into the pastoral elegiac convention and has conceived of another possible consolation (that is, the strewing of the hearse or bier with flowers, as mainly the grave is strewn elsewhere in the tradition), he is struck by its unreality. As his contemplation of the possible rescue of Lycidas by his Muse or guardian angel was interrupted by the realisation that even in myth (let alone in the reality of drowning) this could not be relied upon (for Calliope was unable to save Orpheus from a still more monstrous fate), so now his resort to the

33

ritual of flower decoration is interrupted by the reality that there can be no hearse to strew, no body. The inadequacy of the flowers, their redundancy, is not, however, total. The thoughts are 'frail' because they 'dally with false surmise' (one recalls sporting with Amaryllis in the shade) rather than facing grief squarely, and yet there is a muted contradiction here with 'For so to interpose a little ease' of the previous line. What is illustrated, perhaps, is human frailty (the inability to 'bear very much reality', in Eliot's words) – for this, with 'our moist vows', is the only place where 'we' seems used of man in general, save for the related 'guerdon' for which 'we hope' in line 73. Whilst the flowers cannot be strewed by the valleys over the hearse in real expression of grief and tribute (the 'moist vows', prayers, are 'deny'd'), yet the idea is permitted by the speaker as by the poet, in order still to interpose the little ease (a respite from grief; or an interlude between St Peter's speech and other solemn matter felt to be impending). Thus, like the reflection on what the nymphs might have done, like (possibly) the mourning of the woods and caves, the image remains, is not excluded from the poem as dramatic portrayal; consolations which are rejected in the light of the 'answer' are not rejected from the poem as a work of art in which the journey is as important as the destination, and Time must be conquered through Time.

Both the intrusions of reality into the poem are prefaced by 'Ay me!' (56, 154), and the one appears to echo the other. The fact of a senseless death by drowning could not have been averted by any conceivable intervention and the mourner cannot be consoled by the Nature which has been exonerated of causing the death. The mourning of all Nature is no sufficient 'meed' for the 'Laureat' whose powers were distinctly beyond Nature so conceived, and the decking of the bier is no satisfaction to the spokesman with a need for expressive tribute, since there is no bier. The body is far from the pastoral world, perhaps in the region of the Hebrides, or of Land's End and St Michael's Mount, which looks towards Spain (England's enemy and the home of the 'wolves'). For the first time since the lament of Nature so much earlier in the poem was summed up as 'Such, Lycidas, thy loss to Shepherd's ear' (49), Lycidas is addressed directly by the speaker:

> Whilst thee the shores and sounding Seas
> Wash far away, where ere thy bones are hurld ...
> Look homeward Angel now, and melt with ruth ...

The 'angel' and 'thee' may or may not be one and the same. It has long been argued[11] that the angel is St Michael, being the patron of seafarers, who is asked to look towards England and 'melt with ruth' for Lycidas's misfortune. This is to make 'Whilst thee the shores ...' a series of clauses dependent on 'let our frail thoughts dally with false surmise', and with 'look homeward Angel...' interjected. Alternatively, a new sentence may begin at 'Whilst thee the shores...', of which 'Look homeward Angel...' is the main clause. In that case, both 'thee' and the angel are most readily taken to be Lycidas. They are then akin to, for instance, Phillisides (in Bryskett's *Pastoral Eclogue* on Sidney), who is invited to 'look down a while from where thou sitst above' and to witness the intensive mourning ceremonials (including the strewing of flowers) which are being performed below as the first of an annual rite: or, indeed, to Hervey in Cowley's poem, who looks down on 'our dull and earthly poesie' with 'holy pity'.[12] This latter reading, which seems more probable syntactically, means that there is no very special object of the 'ruth' or pity, unless it refers to the general state of things in the homeland and in particular the state of affairs commented on by St Peter. The analogies, however, suggest that 'ruth' may at least partly refer to the misery of the bereaved and the inadequacy of their consolations; it is not far from the pious flowers of Bryskett's poem, 'which faded, show the givers faded state' (and also 'their fervent zeale and pure') as they are strewn on the grave, to the flowers in the mind of Milton's speaker which cannot be strewn because there is no bier or grave. But, however these lines are taken, it seems plain that they represent both the intrusion of the uncompromising reality of death (its purposelessness shown by the wanderings of the bones) and the hazy emergence of a vision transcending the natural order. As the 'great vision of the guarded Mount' prepares poetically for the angel, so the angel, whether or not 'thee', prepares for the vision of Lycidas outside the pastoral setting. It is almost as if the poignant realisation of the absence of the corpse were a necessary preliminary to the realisation of the presence of the spirit.

The presence of the spirit is dual, corresponding to the immediate reality of the pagan pastoral ('genius of the shore') and to the higher reality which the speeches of Phoebus and St Peter have suggested. The apotheosis, the Christian consolation, has been prepared for by the lofty conception of these speeches, by the angel (whether or not Lycidas) and by the strands of imagery which pervade the poem. Lycidas is literally 'sunk beneath the watry floar', rather than floating 'upon his watry bear Unwept' and at the mercy of the winds (a pastoral fancy akin to that of the hearse which might have been strewn with flowers). We see now why the 'head' which was 'sunk low' by the 'perfidious bark' (102) is indeed to be considered 'sacred' – what appeared exaggerated claims of convention now appear justified by the apotheosis, itself conventional. The 'sacred head' is as the 'day-star' (perhaps the sun but, more commonly in pastoral elegy, Phosphor (Lucifer)/Hesper, the planet Venus setting and rising).[13] Its appearing 'in the forehead of the morning sky' recalls 'the opening eyelids of the morn' (26) under which the shepherds had driven a field, and also 'the star that rose at evening, bright' (30). It is a resurrection after the manner of and with the aid of 'Him that walk'd the waves', that is, Christ of *Matthew* xiv. But it is a resurrection of a kind also for the speaker's spirits, the desired consolation, for the efforts of St Peter (who in the poem represents the values of the speaker and Lycidas) to walk the waves were unsuccessful until Christ stretched forth his hand to him. (It might also be implied that unassisted efforts to reform the corruption in the fold will not succeed either.) Similarly, the efforts of the speaker to make sense of this death, not only to salve grief but as much to find justice, in pastoral terms have been unsuccessful without a divine intervention.

The consolation, the vision, comes, though with some surprise (even after the rather weak invocation of the dolphins), yet without the flash of a mystical experience and the struggle for words to explain it (which is a feature of later poems). Perhaps modern taste would be suited by more of ratiocination (to use Johnson's word) in the step from the bones being hurled in the stormy Hebrides to the saintly figure annointed with (pagan) nectar and with the tears being wiped from his eyes in apocalyptic manner. But even if the tears are connected with the angel's 'ruth', to give some poetic continuity, there seems the suggestion that ultimately there can be no continuity; it is a question of all or nothing, of walking on the waves or sinking, and the faith is absolute. There is both in the movement of the verse and in the assured eclecticism of the imagery, as well as in the step from what in the religious sense is near to despair, the weight of accepted belief, a consolation which the poet can rely on his reader to appreciate – a reliance not available to the Nineteenth Century elegists.

This vision is paralleled by a consolation of practical benefit on the pastoral earth. By virtue of his elevation, Lycidas becomes a 'genius of the shore' more effective to those 'that wander in the perilous flood' than could have been the nymphs in 'the remorseless deep'. The power he gains by virtue of his 'large recompense' – the appointment as genius of the shore is a sort of generous overflowing of his promotion. The ship is of course a traditional image of the body passing through the sea of life – Henry King in fact developed the theme in his contribution to the memorial volume. The 'fatall and perfidious bark' may therefore be tentatively taken to refer to the physical world (associated here with conventional pastoral 'nature' until the apotheosis) as opposed to the world in which Edward King is claimed to have moved, to the self-dedication of the speaker, the values of the two 'digressionary' speeches. Whilst it seems stretching fancy, and the convention, to suggest that King would, in this new form, literally be of much avail to sailors, it is not impossible to see him, by his inspiration, assisting those adrift in the perilous flood of everyday reality.

One such voyager through life is, of course, the 'uncouth swain', which conceivably includes a reference both to the then unknown Milton (whose initials alone appeared with the poem and who, even if the poem had been commissioned, might not come readily to the minds of its intended readers, but who might equally mean to stress that his contribution, as was his connection, was modest) and to the ancient tradition of poetic modesty by which the most learned of poets have delighted in sophisticated ways of clothing their work with the appearance of a rough spontaneity. (The 'dialect' of Spenser's *Shepheardes Calendar* is a case much to the point.) There seems to be a considerable clash between the 'uncouth swain' with his 'Dorick lay', on the one hand, and the mosaic of allusions and images and carefully placed rhetorical devices which we have just been reading, on the other (not to mention the 'swain's' knowledge of the New Testament and contemporary Church matters). Johnson did not fail to make memorable note of the incongruity between a simple telling of 'how a shepherd had lost his companion' and the decking it 'with a long train of mythological imagery, such as a college easily supplies', though he liked neither tale nor decoration. But the clash, we can now see, is a successful part of the poem in two respects, in that it reemphasises what has already been noted of the gap between the heavenly and pastoral worlds (namely that it is absolute), and in that it draws attention to the poem as monument or artefact.

At the most obvious level, it is plain that the uncouth swain who softly (and traditionally) pipes out the evening, catches up his coat and thinks of the next day, is as much at one with himself as, in the beginning, unseasonably plucking berries, driven by bitter constraint to violate that with which his life should be united and on which it depends, he was at odds. Time, certainly, has passed, but the poem does not refer to the attractions of oblivion or the healing of time itself. The salving is rather a process of argument culminating in a step beyond argument to faith. Death brought the thought, primarily, of the purposelessness of effort, when the dedicated and self-indulgent seemed alike subject to the whims of Atropos with the shears. Then again, it brought to mind the vocation of Lycidas–King and the precisely parallel notion that the 'wolves' seemed to get on as well as those dedicated in this direction. Both reflections concluded in a vision of 'account' and Judgment in which the preferred values were believed to triumph. Finally, death brought – simply loss, the sense of eternal separation conveyed by 'Whilst thee the shore and sounding Seas Wash far away', and to that the answer was the largest assertion of faith, embracing the other two, Lycidas recognised in heaven and influential, representing the capability of these virtues to triumph on earth by example. With this resolution, the swain has cause to twitch his mantle.

37

But that is only one aspect of the effect which the return to the uncouth swain may have upon us. We have noted the compulsion under which the monody (but not necessarily also the poem) is uttered, a compulsion it may seem, not only – if, in fact, very much at all – of grief, but also of duty. The memorable nature of the last two lines of the poem is due to their effect of casualness and also to the swain's solitude (for whether he addresses the 'woeful shepherds' in reality or in his mind, he seems alone during the poem and nowhere more so than at the end). Twitching of a coat suggests catching it up, perhaps twirling it round. It is not quite a shrug of the shoulders, yet there is that in it. 'Tomorrow to fresh Woods, and Pastures new' may convey that 'it's all in the day's work'. The monody is not only (even for its utterer, and certainly not for the poet) an utterance under pressure of grief, permitting a plausible waywardness of structure, but it is also a dutiful memorial, the 'meed' or 'lucky words' which the poet or speaker would not be ashamed to have at his own dying. Therefore the appearance of random digression is, from the poet's point of view and perhaps also from that of the speaker, a calculated illusion, and the inadequacy of the pagan pastoral (of which so much of the poem consists) is built in as a sort of virtuoso effect. (We are coming closer to Edward Lear.) In particular, there is the self-consciousness of the artist, Milton and speaker shiftingly as one, suggesting the duty to perform the *pastoral* lament and the insistent intrusion of a reality whose problems are insufficiently covered by the embellished rustic world alone. There is no simple equation of Amaryllis with the pastoral, and of the 'homely slighted shepherd's trade' with the world of spiritual values, for it is a 'shepherd' who speaks of both. But the comparison is among the many references, overt and implicit, to the poet's art – that is, to his career, and to his making. The 'oate proceeds', as it were, to the task of the moment, the ensuring that Lycidas shall not float unwept, and yet that task cannot be completed without for a while dealing with a 'higher mood' and a 'dread voice', and a consolation which will end the mourning. The latter are, perhaps, improbable, from the 'uncouth swain' shepherd, but not from that other 'shepherd', the poet; Milton's acceptance of the conventional analogy is more, rather than less, than it superficially seems, for he and his 'swain' are both shepherds, and neither totally separate nor fully identified.

It follows that we cannot assume that the more 'pastoral' pieces are to be regarded as the work of the 'swain' without the poet's endorsement and that the more probing reflections are the work of Milton the poet, rather as if sections of one tape were spliced in between sections of another. They are all conceived as the monody of the one speaker of 'eager thought'. Although the pastoral 'streams' are 'shrunk' by the 'dread voice', and the strewing of the flowers (which elsewhere is normally offered in good faith as a working tribute and expression) is inapplicable to the speaker's grief, we can reject neither level of the poem. We are obliged to see the whole from outside, as it is from inside, as the product of necessity and memorial duty. This is not, surely, impossible. There is, there cannot be, any antithesis between 'real passion' and Ariel dressing up in the robes of Prospero, unless we have an extraordinarily narrow notion of what constitutes real passion. The allusion to Lear may, I think, be put down to puckish exaggeration, but that the peom was conceived as a triumph of 'invention', of art mingled with artifice, seems undeniable. We come back to the fact that the fancy's interposing a little ease is valid and essential for the poem, even if purely for the argument of the speaker it is rejected. *Lycidas* is in the tradition of what its speaker has chosen to call dallying with false surmise – that of the flower of poetry for bier or tombstone.

III

Gray
Elegy Written In a Country Churchyard

On several counts Gray's *Elegy* is the odd one out among the elegies considered in this book. It is not directly part of the tradition of pastoral elegy going back to Theocritus and, more importantly, it does not extensively refer to that tradition (as, for example, does *In Memoriam*), suggesting that it wishes to be regarded as a modern equivalent or complement to pastoral elegy. In fact, it is not clearly an elegy at all, in the sense of a lamentation for the loss of one man, particularly a poet, cut off 'ere his prime', or a memorial for such a person. The title, 'Elegy', was apparently the second, or even later, thought of Gray, and precisely what prompted it we do not know, though it clearly refers to *lacrimae rerum*,[1] a regret for the disparity between the human condition as it is observed to be and as it might more ideally be conceived. In the manuscript the poem was entitled 'Stanzas wrote in a Country Churchyard'; before publication it was referred to as 'The Stanzas', and the title 'Elegy' was given to it on Gray's insistence, but according to Mason (his friend and not entirely reliable biographer) at Mason's prior persuasion. 'Reflections in a Country Churchyard' was another candidate, though not, it seems, with Gray's approval.[2]

The poem incorporates no invocation, procession of mourners, nor the tribute of flowers (though some form of the latter had been written and was excluded by Gray). It is not about shepherds, or beings disguised as shepherds, whether of Sicily, Arcady or of anywhere else. It has no consolation in the conventional sense (though it has a resolution) because it hardly centres on loss, though a consolation and the search for it was, after *Lycidas*, to be a fairly normal constituent in a traditional elegiac piece. While indeed it includes a certain amount of 'natural description' in a functional way, the 'natural' setting *is* (in the poem as we now have it) primarily a setting and not a theme in itself. Gray did not like descriptive verse as such; he could admire description as ornament (in which one would think there were degrees) and presumably where, as here, it had structural purpose, but 'I have always thought that it made the most graceful ornament of poetry, but ought never to make the subject'.[3] There is an important sense in which Nature mourns, but it is not a matter of buds falling in spring and dried grass being useless to the sheep. Ostensibly, then, the pastoral is irrelevant or (which could be the same thing) dead, and it is a poem entirely in a contemporary mode, a generalised product of an age of prose –

> The woods of Arcady are dead,
> And over is their antique joy;
> Of old the world on dreaming fed;
> Grey Truth is now her painted toy.[4]

Yet, if the poem at so many points fails to follow the conventions, why are we considering it here? The answer is partly that no study of major English elegies could well omit it. But it is also, and more importantly, that in its essentials Gray's *Elegy* touches this tradition at many points, and consideration of them is of interest both to appreciation of the poem and to seeing how, although the formulae, the *topoi*, of the convention of pastoral elegy are no longer precisely followed, they become in the later tradition essential points of reference. That is why we may move from the term 'convention' to that of 'tradition' – a broader thing and also partly a retrospective thing. Gray's *Elegy* has an important place in this development.

But first, before considering the poem, we must deal with what might otherwise be a distraction, or lead to the notion of a closer relationship with the other poems than can be shown to exist. It might be thought that if a personal origin for the poem could be clearly established, it would become a clearer and a better work of art – or at least that some true potential would be realised. I think that this idea should be resisted, though not at the cost of insisting exclusively on a completely contrary view. Briefly, the circumstances surrounding the poem are that in June 1742 Gray's friend and literary correspondent West, the subject of his problematic *Sonnet on the Death of Mr Richard West*,[5] died of consumption, aged 25 (as was Gray). Here, particularly since in Gray there was alleged to be 'an affectation in delicacy, or rather effeminacy',[6] and the two had been friends since their school-days at Eton, might appear to be material for a lachrymatory effusion commemorating a relationship which time had cut short, but which no extension of time could have seen to fulfilment, or perhaps (nearer to what we have) a controlled and distant expression of brave affection. (Such conceptions may, of course, arise with any of these poems but, as I have said, there are other reasons for the urgency of elegies

41

purporting to mourn male associates and colleagues.)

Yet the evidence of a close and contemporary connection between West's death and the *Elegy* is very far from conclusive. Mason believed that the poem was written in 1742 in its first version, with a stoical conclusion arguing for an influence of the 'sacred calm' of evening, 'a grateful earnest of eternal peace', on the mind of the speaker, 'before the happy idea of the hoary-headed Swain, Etc. suggested itself to him.' He thought it was concerned with West. There is nothing finally to refute the idea, though, in this version, one cannot feel that there is internal evidence to support it. The manuscript is quite compatible with the notion of a first version ending in this way and then taken up later for the addition of the present conclusion from 'Far from the madding crowd's ignoble strife' onwards. But, unfortunately, apart from Mason's words and the appeal of sentiment, there is nothing strongly in favour of the association either, and, on his own admission, the 'happy idea' of the ending which would best connect with West's death was not written in 1742 anyway. Mason did not know Gray until about 1747, after the time concerned, and may well be going by inference – he is 'inclined to believe' that the first version was written in 1742.

Walpole, who of course had been a close friend of Gray earlier but was estranged from him at the time of West's death, might be thought the stronger witness, and he believed that the poem dates from 'at least three or four years' after West's death. But Walpole, who communicated this view to Mason, may have had his own reasons for saying that Mason's (lost) reply, presumably upholding Mason's opinion, put an end to his criticism of Mason's dating; he could have wished to cool down an argument between them on the way in which Mason's *Memoirs* handled his (Walpole's) relationship with Gray. Again, Gray himself stated in 1750 that Walpole had seen the poem 'long ago' and Walpole said that he had seen its 'twelve or more first lines' in 1746 – but he could hardly have seen any version before 1745 (as Mason's lost reply may have reminded him) since it was not till then that he became reconciled with Gray. In default of evidence that Gray for some reason deliberately showed him less than was actually written, or that Walpole actually saw more than he says, we are thus driven to conclude from this that the poem was newly written in about 1746 in one or other form, four years after West's death. Finally, Gray's letter of 12th June, 1750, which says that Walpole has seen the beginning 'long ago', makes a definite play about the rest, complete with ending, which he is sending him now; 'and having put an end to a thing, whose beginning you have seen long ago, I immediately send it you. You will, I hope, look upon it, in the light of a thing with an end to it . . .' This play on 'end' does seem to suggest that the end is somehow notable over and above whatever Walpole had seen before, and that it is freshly written;

42

it may be everything but the first twelve lines, or it may be the 'ending', as we now have it rather than the 'first version' which can be conjecturally constructed from the manuscript and from Mason's remarks.

These matters[7] would not need to be recited were it not that they point to a mystery about the *Elegy* which has always exercised its critics. While the precise date of the poem may not matter to some, except for biographical reasons and to establish what works by others might have influenced the poem, and while also it can be held that a poem should be read for what it is independently of its precipitating circumstances, there remains an enigma at the core of the *Elegy* as to the extent to which personal underlies apparently impersonal, to which general embodies particular. This is a part of the substance, the way in which the reader is directed, rather than a peripheral matter. It would not be resolved, but I think it would be naive to bow to the theory to such an extent as to say that it would not be affected, by any settlement of the date and relations of the poem.

In part, of course, this is a matter we have already considered in connection with *Lycidas*; if Johnson had not known that the poem was in some sense a personal elegy for King, would he still have objected so strongly to the 'fiction' and the 'little grief'? Would he not rather have related *Lycidas* to classical pastorals whose personal content was not on the whole known and presumed to be slight, and have come down a little more – for Johnson was no lover of pastoral anyway – in the poem's favour? Alternatively, if we knew nothing of Hallam, what would we make of *In Memoriam*? In Gray's *Elegy*, however, there seems to be a more radical difficulty; we seem to be presented with a feeling which might be both personal and general, which might never have been closely personal, or which, being essentially deeply personal, has been deliberately 'distanced' by diction and structural device (as, perhaps, has been the feeling of the *Sonnet* on West's death). And Johnson, of course, as a sort of afterthought in a *Life of Gray* which as a whole leaves an impression not far short of distaste, commended it; 'In the character of his *Elegy* I rejoice to concur with the common reader . . . *The Churchyard* abounds with images which find a mirror in every mind, and with sentiments to which every bosom returns an echo . . .'

What are these 'images' and 'sentiments' of which Johnson so approved and which on the face of it might be the barest clichés? They are particularly, it would seem, those of the 'first version' (that is, those of the first 92 lines of the poem as we now have it) without its conclusion, lines which may appear to come directly from the poet, as opposed to the more dramatised 'ending' which is closer in some ways to the tradition of *Lycidas*. In this first part are depicted elements of a rural scene of which

43

the key is the fading of external objects until the speaker is alone in a sort of hushed suspense – 'And all the Air a solemn stillness holds' – a situation we shall meet again in later poems. The day is 'parting', the 'herd' is winding slowly home, the ploughman plodding in the same direction, and the landscape is fading from sight. The folds lulled by 'tinkling' are distant, the beetle is 'droning', traditionally drowsy, and the owl complains because her 'solitary reign' is disturbed. All conspires to a suspension of animation, a peace absolute without ingredient save for 'stillness', and, as external things withdraw, we depend on 'me' for the relief of a tension in the solemn stillness, for 'me' to create and fill the void. As Marvell puts it, in 'this delicious solitude' the mind' Withdraws into its own happiness . . . Yet it creates'. What it creates, for Gray as for Marvell, is a realisation of 'that happy Garden state' – life in Eden and, inevitably, a recognition of the fallen state in comparison.

It is, then, with the introduction by the solitary mind of questions of value that the rural and topographical becomes the 'pastoral' of contrasted ways of life, with the weight finally in favour of the simple and the elemental but, in Gray's poem, the retention of a complex and delicate balance. That introduction occurs in the lines

> Each in his narrow cell for ever laid,
> The rude forefathers of the hamlet sleep.

The 'narrow' suggests mean poverty and, with 'for ever', the reflection of a perpetuated injustice which is reinforced by 'rude'. The 'cell' suggests imprisonment by death in a humble state for which there should, perhaps, have been no necessity, and yet 'sleep' offers the cognate perpetuation of peace – far from the madding crowd; there is a gain and a loss in the obscurity of the poor. The 'hamlet' is more lowly even than the 'village', which was Gray's earlier word. (The change was probably influenced by a leaning to Milton's L'Allegro (92) and Il Penseroso which, perhaps significantly with regard to the question of personal loss, were more influential on the Elegy than was Lycidas.)

The following lines extend these initial suggestions of value. The 'rude forefathers' are associated with domestic contentment, joy, noise and activity, awakened by the swallows and 'the cock's shrill clarion or the echoing horn', and coming home to a 'blazing hearth' and a 'busy' wife with whom the lisping children compete to kiss. The work was 'jocund' and the felling strokes 'sturdy'. Here, it would seem, is a selection of values which idealises, whether or not justifiably, village agricultural life beyond what can have been the general reality. On the other hand, in appearance these 'short and simple annals' are trivial enough, and to them are opposed the more impressive 'Ambition' and 'Grandeur', as opposition which is essentially false or insignificant since

44

> *'all that beauty, all that wealth e'er gave*
> *Awaits alike the inevitable hour'* (34–5)

– and since, we are perhaps to suppose (as most notably does William Empson in *Some Versions of Pastoral*), the equality of man in the face of death is an intimation of what equality there should ideally be in life. This contrast of earthly 'glory' and 'the grave' appears to bring the speaker's thoughts back to the 'narrow cell', with which he compares the lavish monuments, the memorial services with 'pealing Anthems', for Ambition and Grandeur. (The 'pealing Anthems' are related to the 'pealing organ' and 'Anthems clear' of *Il Penseroso* (161–3), as are the outward signs of Fame, as against levelling death, to the discussion of Fame in *Lycidas*.) It is notable here, from the point of view of idealisation, that 'Ambition' and 'Grandeur' (in themselves one would have thought neutral qualities) are paralleled to 'ye Proud' and, whilst 'Honour's voice' as an epitaph may be unobjectionable, 'Flatt'ry' plainly is not; the speaker seems not to see in the mighty the possibility of recognisable merits, such potential as he next, returning to the 'narrow cell' in the 'neglected spot', proceeds to impute as often unrecognisable in the humble.

On the one hand, Gray idealises the poor of the hamlet, making them representative of a sort of quietism which is valued highly in the poem and corresponds to the mental state to which the speaker has for a moment attained. On the other hand, he declares that their situation is unfulfilled and implies, perhaps, some social injustice. It will not do in our reading of the poem to elevate one of these aspects of the poor over the other, no matter which. It may appear that the unrealised virtues of these people are suppressed by an apparently ameliorable situation, for 'chill Penury', an economic problem, 'froze the genial current of the soul'. But the poem is not, I think, concerned with whether that problem can be or even should be solved. It would seem that the 'gem of purest ray serene' (one recalls the true Fame, the jewel without need of 'glistering foil', in *Lycidas*, 78) is nonetheless a jewel, and the blushing rose no less a rose, for being unseen to be so; the impression is that it requires the omniscience of God, or the limited omniscience of the artist, to record these unrecognised qualities – this is a central theme underlying the *Elegy*.[8]

The unrecognised virtues must, one would think, correspond to unrecognised vices (the 'frailties' as well as the 'merits' at the end of the poem are beyond reach). But that is not how Gray puts it here. Having considered hypothetical human analogies to the gem and the flower (that is, the Hampdens, Miltons and Cromwells who never emerged), he then states that the 'lot' which 'circumscribed' the virtues also 'their crimes confin'd'. This, in connection with the jewel and the rose, is a convenient but rather a curious development, for the virtues of these symbols were

45

essentially existent but unrecognised. But now it seems to be implied that the recognition of the 'virtue' (or the vice) is in part a condition of its 'growing' – that in the circumspection of the unrecognised potential of the heroes was a limitation of their true quality, their essential Fame (in the sense offered by Phoebus in *Lycidas*). We face the paradox that that which is concealed, peaceful, withdraw, is good and untarnished (but possibly ineffective). If it is not good, it is at least limited. That which is public, showy, ambitious is at least suspect, and probably not good. Although it is a great loss that there should be mute inglorious Miltons, retirement is a positive thing and the qualities of the gem and the rose subsist without being seen (from which it is a short step to feeling that they depend on not being seen); but meanwhile both the virtues and the vices are felt to be limited by their obscurity.

Here Gray, in his first version (if that it was) moved towards the apparent ending which was subsequently excluded, and in it he emphasised the association of the unrecognised with a positive value of peace. In sum, this quality, which plainly belongs to the 'rude forefathers', is declared to be 'Innocence', a virtue to which in practice more is owed by the 'thoughtless world' than is owed to 'majesty', 'the brave' and 'success'. The speaker ends as he began, with his 'lonely Contemplation', 'sacred calm' and 'eternal Peace'. The gem lost in the subterranean cave, the forefathers sleeping in their tombs, and the speaker in the dark silence of the graveyard, all are woven into one – so much so that the lines referred at one stage, by a rather Freudian slip, to the speaker's relation with his own ('thy') 'artless Tale', rather than to 'their artless tale' – that of the 'unhonour'd dead' in general. The description of the neglected poor in the poem as we have it now –

> Along the cool sequestered vale of life
> They kept the noiseless tenor of their way (75–6)

– was in this first version an instruction of the speaker to himself, to imitate the modest virtues and to 'pursue the silent Tenor of thy doom' along a similarly sequestered vale.

We may, I think, take it that the foregoing are in the main the 'images which find a mirror in every mind' and 'sentiments to which every bosom returns an echo'. They comprise some form of idealisation of an agricultural community which is also, problematically, pitied. Its values are not clamant nor even, it is suggested, in their essence apparent, and they are opposed to those of the public and celebrated world outside, much as, a decade or two ago, 'history' consisted of dates and heroes rather than of the everyday life of the people. There is some conflict between the concepts of genuine virtues which cannot come to light because of their 'lot' (which it may or may not be practicable to change without losing the

46

concomitant values), virtues more actual which may be felt to depend upon this social situation, and virtues which, like demerits, are 'circumscribed' by the 'lot'. But there is certainly an essential connection between obscurity and value, and both are found with the rural poor rather than with the ostentation which the 'inevitable hour' will in due course level. And, finally, the speaker becomes identified with the values which he assigns to the dead forefathers. They are (as they were in life like the unknown gem) one with their surroundings, the 'solemn stillness' with which the poem began and with which, in this version, it ends in 'sacred calm'. He who has realised the import of this calm is adjusted by the process, and adjusted (the turn to address the self as 'thee' suggests) by the very process of thought or the utterance, which is itself presumed to be influenced by the surroundings. He becomes, or can conceive of becoming, 'no more with Reason and thyself at strife', may pursue with a clear conscience a 'silent tenour' – a way related, perhaps, to meditating the thankless muse in *Lycidas* – since he is assured that virtue and value may exist 'noiseless', independent of recognition.

But Johnson, though his conclusions were perhaps based principally on the first part of the poem, was not thinking solely of the 'first version', and he did not quite stop short at general praise. He went on to say that 'the four stanzas beginning "Yet even these bones" are to me original; I have never seen the notions in any other place; yet he that reads them here persuades himself that he has always felt them.' Here, with his infallible eye or ear for the crux of a matter, Johnson picks on the turning point of the poem as it is now known. It is because he does so that we know that 'images that find a mirror in every mind' have appealed to him in a way different from when (of the *Prospect of Eton College*) he might appear to be saying the same thing, in condemnation – it 'suggests nothing to Gray which every beholder does not equally think and feel'. For these quoted lines mark the beginning of a change of direction in the *Elegy*. They begin to imply what we have noted as a recurrent theme in pastoral elegy and what very soon after them emerges fully. I mean, of course, the idea of the memorial that is needed and has not yet been made, the necessity for the 'meed of some melodious tear' as in *Lycidas*, an idea no more than faintly implicit in Gray's poem as apparently first conceived. They suggest that one resolution of 'Reason and thyself at strife', one intimation of 'eternal Peace', would be the construction of such a 'memorial'. In the paradox of the jewel and flower unrecognised or undeveloped, they prepare for the emphasis to shift heavily towards the celebration of the truth which, for whatever reason, goes unnoticed in life.

We have already had contrasted the 'storied urn or animated bust' with the 'narrow cell' and 'neglected spot'. To a large extent, the difference

47

between them is just; proud monuments commemorate that which cannot 'really' last without the aid of these props, show commemorates show and is as nothing before the fact of death. But to a degree also, the difference is too large – to the degree that, in these lines, it is a human instinct to call for memorial, and the 'shapeless sculpture' and so forth (or nothing) do not adequately recognise either this call or the unseen qualities of the gem. The universal urge to memorial is preceded by the word 'yet', because it might be the assumption that such as these in fact require no memorial at all, being self-sufficient as rose and jewel. 'Yet' this is not so, 'for who was so forgetful that he left life behind' (or, less probably, 'for who was so attracted by death – "dumb Forgetfulness" – that he left life behind') 'without casting back a look of regret (one recalls Orpheus) at the cheerful day' – a day still 'cheerful' to the poor? The forefathers are not exempt from this cry for memorial. 'It is impossible to conquer that natural desire we have of being remembered' Mason refers to Gray as noting.[9] The uncouth and 'frail memorial' with its rustic moral and bizarre sculpture supplies a token, but not the due of the forefathers. It is left, ironically, to the poet to construct the latter, a more potent monument than either the storied urns or the shapeless masonry.

So, by way of the same (adapted) lines in which, in the early version, Gray inadvertently identified 'thee' (the speaker) and 'thy/their artless tale', making explicit the association of speaker and rural poor which was anyway implicit, the speaker turns to an example, 'thee', who is the subject of the rest of the poem. It seems to me beyond doubt that 'thee' represents primarily the speaker addressing himself. That would be the natural extension of the first version where he does the same. There is nothing 'mawkish'[10] in this unless, of course, we go on to sentimentalise the poet's life, at a time which we cannot with precision identify, in terms of what little we learn of the 'youth'. Furthermore, to say that the speaker is 'thee' is not to identify the speaker with the poet, though it would be unreasonable to find no connection between them. 'Thee', whilst he must have a good deal in common with the carver of the 'shapeless culpture' and framer of the rustic moral, cannot (without a sense of tortuous ingenuity at variance with the broad and simple lines of the poem as a whole) be taken as some imported village poet or sculptor, author not only of the frail memorials but also of what follows.[11] I take it also that the 'artless tale', whilst referring ironically to the 'uncouth rhymes' on the tombstones as being of the same species, refers to the poem itself, imagined as a monologue. The self-disparagement of the poet is as much a feature of pastoral elegy and its tradition as is a discussion of the merits of the form and its art (is, indeed, part of the same thing). We have already noted in *Lycidas* the suggestion of the elegy as a rather burdensome necessity, a bitter-sweet responsibility, the contrast of the 'oat' and the 'higher mood', the artful artlessness of the uncouth swain. It is surely on this basis, with a putative identity of the mourner and the mourned, that the second part of Gray's *Elegy* moves, and it would be entirely appropriate if the 'youth' who is elegised were the speaker or poet as much as, or more than, West, just as the speaker of *Lycidas* (19–20) had pondered on the idea of an elegy for himself.[12] Most probably, and regardless of when the poem was first written, 'thee' and the 'youth' are at once the speaker, Gray, and West, involved in whatever experience of death (and certainly that, in his family, was manifold) Gray had had.

The dead 'youth to Fortune and to fame unknown' is clearly and importantly akin to the unhonoured dead and those of 'destiny obscure' who lack elegy or 'fame'. His virtues, like those of the gem, were potential, or at least undisplayed, since he, like Lycidas, is 'dead ere his prime'; they existed, the Epitaph declares, the bulk of them known only to God, for the youth had no 'sudden blaze' of glistering foil. In details also, the end of the *Elegy* recalls *Lycidas*. The 'hoary-headed swain', who might enquire after this unknown being's fate, would recall seeing him 'at peep of dawn' (98 – cf. *Lycidas* 26, 'Under the opening eyelids of the morn'), meeting 'the sun upon the upland lawn' (100 – cf. *Lycidas* 25, 'ere the high lawns appeared'; *L'Allegro* 92, 'upland hamlets' – it was this that possibly led to the change from 'village' to 'hamlet' at the start of the *Elegy*), and 'brushing with hasty steps the dews away' (99 – *Lycidas* 29, 'the fresh dews', but in fact 'of night').

What we are concerned with is less the identity of 'thee' with 'Gray' or 'West', than the identity of 'thee' with the speaker (and through him, with those celebrated in the first part), who has a good deal of Gray and West in him. Thus, the fact that the passage draws on several sources, including Shakespeare, for its description of the melancholy man (the wise and sensitive, beginning to approach the Romantic outcast visionary) does not affect the relevance of Gray's description of himself to Walpole in just such a situation. What we then have is, I think, a 're-creation' of the type already mentioned, a recollection of the past to sustain it in the present, and that it should merge with literary precedents is neither a detraction nor surprising.

> (*Burnham Beeches*) *is a little chaos of Mountains and Precipices . . . both Vale and Hill is cover'd over with most venerable Beeches . . . At the foot of one of these squats me I; il Penseroso . . . like Adam in Paradise, but commonly without an Eve . . .*
>
> (Letter to Walpole, Sept. 1737)[13]

It seems entirely reasonable to see a parallel between this passage and the 'youth' lying 'at the foot of yonder nodding beech' in the *Elegy*, provided we do not go on to assume the absolute and sole identity of youth, speaker and Gray, thus giving the poem a more specific application than, so far as is known, can generally be supported. The indebtedness, or at least paralleling, of the *Elegy* to *Il Penseroso* is notable, both as to manner of description and the value ascribed to 'melancholy', and also in point of detail.[14] This similarity reinforces the analogy to Gray's letter, which is not lessened by the possible reference of the lines in the poem to melancholy Jacques in *As You Like It*.[15]

Besides the question of the speaker and his identity with the object of his mourning, there are two further points which may help us to see the poem as related to the *Lycidas* tradition. In the stanza which Gray omitted from his final version, the so-called 'redbreast' stanza –

> *There scatter'd oft, the earliest of the Year,*
> *By hands unseen, are show'rs of Violets found;*
> *The Redbreast loves to build and warble there,*
> *And little footsteps lightly print the ground –*

– there is a condensed 'flower passage'. It is not a 'false surmise', for the speaker is not obviously seeking, nor deprived of, consolation for an intimate loss (the 'swain' who tells the tale of the youth seems little more than an eyesight acquaintance, though he progresses from being one of a group to 'One morn I missed him'), but rather a memorial by 'hands unseen' and an adoption of the youth into innocent Nature. The 'hands unseen' are an extension of the theme of the obscure remembered by the obscure. I am not suggesting that this stanza should have been included – although it occasionally is included in popular prints of the poem. In fact, its inclusion rather spoils this part of the poem, for it makes an unjustified break between 'Approach and read' and the reading of the Epitaph and, perhaps more importantly, it is an unlikely interpolation from the swain, who is (unlike his interlocutor) unable to read. But it does give a further indication of the poem's partial context. Then, secondly, there is the 'fav'rite tree' (which is not in *Lycidas* but appears in Milton's other pastoral elegy, *Epitaphium Damonis*), in this case an ancient beech which must be visible from the churchyard and perhaps contrasts with the 'yew-tree's shade' at the beginning of the poem. Whether or not it is based on reality, the tree appears to owe something to Virgil's *Eclogue II*, where the lovesick Corydon throws off some artless songs among the beechtrees (the letter on Burnham Beeches goes on to say that Gray used to read Virgil in this favourite spot), and it is the forerunner of such notable trees as the 'signal elm' in *Thyrsis* and the sycamore in *In Memoriam*.

'The Epitaph' must have been a very considerable problem to compose, even in an age which made a cult of epitaphs and inscriptions for seats and urns and the like, for it has so many decorums to serve. It had to correspond to the values assigned to those other 'unhonour'd dead'. It had, in a good poem, to be good – alternatively, it might be bad in a way which was quite certainly justified by the dramatic context rather than being the result of the poet's blundering. Since the merits of the rude forefathers were hidden as the hidden gem and the stress was on their modest and regular working and domestic life, it could also make no claims for the deceased's outstanding and unrecognised distinction. It required a moral to 'teach the moralist to dye'. But, despite all this, it could not, plainly, dismiss its subject, whether he were the speaker (as opposed to the enquirer who reads it out) or Gray or West or (more probably) a bit of all three.

In fact, a very good balance is struck. The cirumstances largely, but not as a copy, match those in the 'artless lines'. The youth is 'to fortune and to fame unknown', but he was educated and melancholy (neither of which would meet the generality of the fathers). He was generous and sincere. In return, 'he gained from Heaven ('twas all he wished) a friend'. This 'friend' we may assume to be the 'kindred spirit' who enquired after him and reads the Epitaph. The friend's 'lonely Contemplation' resembles the activity of the youth 'hard by yon wood', and also of the speaker (particularly, of course, as regarded in the 'first version', where he is more prominent in the whole). It may be noted that, whilst clearly there is no precise analogy, the giving of the 'friend' to the 'youth' as a sort of reward parallels the reward to Lycidas – 'Heaven did a recompense as largely send' to the youth, and Lycidas is to be 'Genius of the shore In thy large recompense' (183–4). Then, as if in ironic acknowledgment of the difficulties of writing such a modest encomium, we are told to ask no more since his merits and frailties 'alike' rest in God. There is indeed nothing especially noteworthy about the Epitaph. There could not be, since it had to represent the 'frail memorial', the insignificant guardian of the remains of one otherwise unhonoured, to represent the minimal commemoration corresponding to the rather senseless but undeniable and irresistable calling of the 'Voice of Nature' from the tomb. The poor who for their circumstances can perform nothing very startling, good or bad, are the hidden gem which remains a gem, though unknown; similarly, he who dies young and unfulfilled had no Fame, save with him who 'pronounces lastly on each deed' (*Lycidas* – 83).

I think that it would be fanciful to assert that there is no biographical problem in Gray's *Elegy*. But what is, I think, equally certain, is that it is part of a tradition (including, of course, a large range of pastoral, non-elegiac poetry) going back beyond *Lycidas* to the classics. It is not quite in the main stream of that tradition, but it alludes to it at some of its most important points. To what extent it is a personal elegy for another person (and, in particular, for West) is uncertain and, if known, would have a considerable bearing on the poem. But it would not greatly affect our perception of this poetic context. The *Elegy* would remain a matter of *lacrimae rerum* by means of a dramatised scene as example, rather than a dramatised search for consolation such a *Lycidas*. It is significant that, whilst in the first version, we return to the speaker and the implications he can draw from his reflections and surroundings, the full version of the poem is, as it were, open-ended; the effect of the utterance upon the speaker is not remarked, the scene is not 'distanced', distinguishing speaker and poet, and the effectiveness of the Epitaph as a resolution of what has been raised is left to the reader to judge for himself.

Yet it can hardly be doubted that there is the notion of consolation by memorial, that the Epitaph is such as makes the dead satisfactorily 'honoured'. It proposes to correct, as does the search for consolation in other poems, a sensed injustice. The poem has insistently stressed the wish for memorial as a fundamental need. 'The unhonour'd dead' appear to be the forefathers and those represented by the gem and the flower. The forefathers, at least, have a 'frail memorial', yet they are still, for their true qualities, 'unhonoured'. The *Elegy* is a memorial to their possible real but hidden virtues, which both reside in their way of life and are also a potential which, because of the 'circumspection' of that way of life, they could not manifest. But we confuse biography and literature if we say that West, for his part, could not be considered 'unhonoured', since he had his well-placed grave by the altar-rail at Hatfield. He may or may not have done when the poem was written – the issue is irrelevant. As West might or might not have been, so the poet himself was certainly 'unhonoured' (until the *Elegy* was published). Being alive, he had no monument, and therefore he too is a candidate for being the 'youth', if the youth 'is' anyone. I think we must conclude that the youth is, first and foremost, an example, to which may be affixed in varying and uncertain degrees the persons of West and Gray and people unknown. The Epitaph celebrates qualities in a very modest way, for good dramatic reasons. But, more to the point, it ends by dwelling on the unknowable virtues (and defects) which must exist regardless of any memorial already made. In this it is like *Lycidas* on Fame, in the context of a real death and, by identification, an imagined death. As *Lycidas* concerns unfulfilment in various spheres (notably those of poetry and the church), so does Gray's *Elegy*. (West as well as Gray wrote poetry and indeed West may have set Gray on the path of writing in English rather than in Latin.) But in the *Elegy* the unfulfilment, though it is measured in terms of the size of tombstones, is not solely that brought about by death, and the size of the tombstones is made to appear a rejected criterion of how the world sees things.

Because there is something in the nature of a class-distinction associated with the rural air of the poem, it can too readily be assumed that the *Elegy* is 'pastoral' because it falsifies our experience of Nature, because it overstates the case – the lisping children were doubtless sometimes over their father's knee, we feel, or the fuel for the 'blazing hearth' ran out. But that is not, surely, the falsification which the poem primarily presents. It would be more apt to say that thunderstorms desecrate churchyards, that solitude can beget self-anguish as well as inner peace. It is true that this is in part nostalgic, sentimental pastoral, but it is justified, as in Milton's, by its proximity (itself stylised in the tower, owl, elms, yewtrees, and so on, a conventional scene) to the elements controlling life and death which are its main concern. It is enough that the churchyard is given an atmosphere which plausibly could be felt to be so – in the first version it is still plainer that we are concerned with a specific instance of, rather than a generalisation of, the effect of surroundings. The forefathers are presented as all virtue because virtue is the question in point and which is so easily overlooked in them, not because they are conceived to have had no vices. One does not construct memorials to a person's demerits. It may be that their qualities, good and bad, were limited by the opportunities provided by their social class, but that is not to say that they are so idealised that Gray would rather do without a Milton neither mute nor inglorious. Although it presents nature with a pacific character and allies with that the local folks, the *Elegy* is not escapist – though it must be admitted that the range of feeling, as reflected in the characterisation of Nature, is limited indeed in comparison with that of *Lycidas*. It has sufficient of a dramatic conception (greatly extended by the changes from the first version) to justify or excuse its partiality. It is concerned fundamentally with the real value of what is commonly obscure and unseen, whether through social system or by early death.

And so we return to the lines about the 'rude forefathers'. 'Sleep' is indeed peaceful, part of the 'solemn stillness'. Yet it also suggests awakening, in tension with 'no more . . .' 'Heaven' and 'his Father and his God' emphasise the same idea (which is much developed in the tradition). But the certainty of immortality does not dispose of the need for living recognition on earth. The 'parting soul' is not a totally 'dying soul', yet its voice cries backwards to life and, by contrast, the bodies in the narrow cells are laid there 'for ever'. Even in the presence of Christian consolation, yet 'ev'n in our ashes live their wonted fires'. 'The paths of glory lead but to the grave' and all are levelled when the 'inevitable hour' meets them but, equally, all rely 'on some fond breast' and require 'some pious drops' (cf. *Lycidas* 14, 'meed of some melodious tear'). The proud and the wealthy have theirs and, for the poem's purpose at least, their tombs are just symbols. But the poor whose style was limited, or the youth cut off before he could make any impression, have not theirs. There is felt to be a sort of afterlife in the memorial and, it may be, a compensation for the world's

53

inability to see the truth during life. Hence, having already 'some frail memorial', these dead may still be 'unhonoured' until properly sung in the poem, and the same would apply to the youth, whoever he be, in the final scene. Thd Epitaph is both the precise equivalent to the simple memorials previously described, and also, by virtue of its content in the poem, it goes beyond them. Then there is, of course, the final irony – that the poem, though including an 'Epitaph' in some sense for its writer, is itself a memorial, to one who in Hardy's phrase 'used to notice such things' (*Afterwards*).

IV

Shelley – *Adonais*

Gray's *Elegy* is one in which a sense of injustice in society is paralleled by a sense that this is part of a larger discrepancy in the scheme of things. It asserts broadly that true qualities do not correspond to appearances and that in society rewards are distributed according to those appearances and accentuate them. It does not, I think, suggest that this inequity can or should be corrected by some social reform. Indeed, the force of the 'natural' setting is rather to imply that the flaw is more deeply within the human predicament. We may never have, for reasons which go beyond the dictates of social class or political system and are finally unspecified, the opportunity for our true qualities to be registered as appearances. Yet, if we had that opportunity, it does not follow that the observed qualities would merit an imposing tomb, for the 'true' is both the quality of one's real, hidden self, and also what is valuable in man, and these may not agree. The judgment, such as is to be inferred from erecting animated busts and suchlike, is not really a judgment within our capabilities. And so the 'merit' and 'frailties' of the youth at the end of the *Elegy* cannot be 'disclosed' further, for they rest 'alike' in the bosom of his God.

This God is, from the point of the poem, notable in two respects. In the first place, he does not appear until the last line, and, in the second, he is, as it were, external, indisputable, a point of reference available and with no need of definition. Gray is writing in a Christian age of a Christian-derived, but perhaps primarily a Deist's, God. His public are unlikely to dispute the sentiments either of a final divine point of reference, or of the absence of any sense of appeal or personal devotion to this deity. His invitation to the reader to enquire no further, to leave it to God, is offered less as consolation in the personal elegiac tradition, than as resolution, a reminder of accepted fact in face of an apparent flaw in the system.

With regard to the form of the poem, that the speaker of the *Elegy* may in large measure be Gray does not alter the fact that the poet changed it from a substantially singular, though dramatised, piece to a conception in which the speaker became one of several personages and the sense of a monologue became somewhat weakened. Whether that made the poem more 'personal', by virtue of the introduction of the 'youth', we could discuss for some time, but certainly in consequence the effect of the churchyard's atmosphere on such a person became subordinate to the example, a youth importantly related to the uncelebrated inhabitants of the hamlet. They and he, recognised uniquely it may be by the omniscience of the poet on earth, can be recognised fully only by the omniscience of the God who was added to the poem.

Though it be granted that they were writing poems nearer to the pastoral tradition of loss, Shelley, Arnold and Tennyson did not share these assumptions, nor, on the whole, did they conceive of their public as sharing them. In their different ways they sought consolation individually, in the hope, no doubt, that the example had general meaning, but nonetheless individually and for the losses which they specify. I deliberately say that 'they' sought consolation. It is a feature of this individualisation that the dramatisation of a situation (the irony, if you like) becomes uncertain. We cannot and need not define very exactly to what extent Milton's 'uncouth swain' and Gray's 'thee' who relates the artless tale are distinct from their creator or representations of their creators, although I suspect that there will always be a wish to go further in the case of Gray's poems than established fact will (at least at present) justify. The duality in these poems appears to be part of the purpose. What we do, and no doubt what their first readers did, is to perceive the possibility of considerable differences, differences which mean we have no *de facto* obligation to identify these people, and which permit us to view the work of art as faceted according as to how it is viewed, independent and complete without reference back to what historically we do not fully know.

But with the Nineteenth Century poets (and notwithstanding the development by Browning of the 'dramatic monologue' in full face of and because of the tendency[1]) the position is different. They are uneasy, in the realm of elegy, as to the relative importance of defining the lost and seeking consolation for the loser (Milton may too have been uneasy, but he transcended the difficulty), though the emphasis falls finally on the loser. There is a mysterious ambivalence (of which the classic example is the contrast between the languid mood and the apparently strenuous exhortation of Tennyson's *Ulysses*, in which 'there is more about myself' under the influence of Hallam's death than there is in *In Memoriam*) in their attitude to the world substituted for the world of loss. They see more interest in the unfulfilment, the incompleteness, of the bereaved than in the mysterious possibility of the fulfilment of the beloved dying ere his prime. Instead of attempting to fit the apparent injustice of death into an accepted larger context in terms of which it may be incomprehensibly just, they attempt on their own to create such a scheme which will make sense of their personal lives, incorporating in it imagery derived on a very wide basis from pagan and Christian mythologies. The inherent connection between an afterlife, or transcendence contingent upon death, and the death-wish, becomes very much more apparent. The desire is for a union, a merging, in the contemplation of which the threatened loss of personal identity appears of minor importance. Above all, they feel loneliness, and they address beings and objects of all sorts, including the departed, to create what sometimes seems an illusion of intercourse and communion. Deeply they yearn, or strenuously strive, to 'leap' or 'jump' the boundaries of mortal and immortal, or animate and inanimate, for true reality, it seems, must be so much vaster than our limited apparent world – if that world is to have any meaning. These are reactions, we may feel, very typical of modern man in his grief, and, as these spokesmen are often not described physically, we take it that they are known to us, that they are closely akin, at the very least, to the poets, who speak as nearly as may be directly to the reader.

The uneasiness as to the status of the person left behind is seen partly in a hesitancy in handling the pastoral form and manner, and its styles, so that the whole can become more than a collection of parts. It seems that the enclosed pastoral world is no longer felt to correspond very vitally with the real world before the 'fall'. The pastoral may be an artificiality of the past referred to in the context of a conception of Nature which is felt to be more realistic, or it may be rather a self-contained portion elaborated with a charmed delight but to be abandoned, far more fully than is the pastoral of *Lycidas*, by the end of the poem. Yet it is true that in the largest sense these are all poems of the pastoral tradition. In all of them in varying degrees, whether the talk is of Cumnor, of Stoke Poges (if that is the *Elegy*'s scene), or of Somersby, to Nature is ascribed at least for a while a partiality which reverts to a golden age. Whether it refers to archetypal 'nature' or to individual childhood or youth, or is suggestive of 'eternal Peace', – as Virgil perhaps made an Arcady of the memories of Theocritus – this partiality, if it does not rule the poem, is at the very least a value most seriously considered. Opposing it increasingly, however, is the need for an ideal closer to the poet's experience as enlarged by a sense of death, or the oppressive city life which has become the norm, or the grimmer implications of geological metamorphosis, and the clash cannot be resolved within the pastoral convention or with a vision of the Christian Paradise-to-be. Within the fictional world of the poem, the spokesman does not clearly begin as a shepherd and neither does he clearly end as one. The old pastoral world is not something in which the poet is willing to immerse himself totally; the nearest we come to that is when 'Arnold'

57

declares that he and Thyrsis once 'assayed' their pipes, and that ends with a very uncertain optimism that the pastoral could still influence life in the great town's roar.

Thus it is significant that *Adonais* begins with a thorough-going attempt to create a pastoral piece conventional in the best sense (though uncertain of location and riddled with gods, goddesses, dreams, splendours and the like, over and above what is to be expected in the form) and ends by seeming to abandon it in favour of a solution, tenuously connected by idea, but totally outside the fiction he has created. It was perhaps in observation of this structural problem that Auden remarked 'Indeed, the only elegy I know of which seems to me a failure is *Adonais*'.[2] Yet Shelley himself approached this task in no idle spirit. He declares that it is 'the least imperfect of my compositions'[3], 'a highly wrought piece of art',[4] though he thought few people would be interested in it or understand it, and he 'wrote, as usual, with a total ignorance of the effect that I should produce'.[5] Whatever we may conclude of its construction, there is in its detail some evidence that he consciously followed Keats's advice to 'be more of an artist and "load every rift" of your subject with ore' (written to Shelley, 16th August, 1820, six months before Keats died), and it is possible that he adopted the Spenserian stanza partly in tribute to Keats, of whom it had been a favourite form.

For the outlines of his 'pastoral' Shelley was indebted to the *Lament for Bion* and to Bion's *Lament for Adonis*, from which he also took some detail and a larger fragment of which he had translated.[6] 'Moschus' (as Shelley believed) had referred to Bion as the second loss of the river Meles (claimed to be the birthplace of both Homer and Bion), and so Shelley conceives of Urania's having suffered the death of Keats following on the loss of Milton:

> *He died*
> *Who was the sire of an immortal strain . . .*
> *But now thy youngest, dearest one, has perished –*
> *The nursling of thy widowhood.*
>
> (*Adonais* 29ff)[7]

'Moschus', again, relates that Bion was poisoned – 'There came poison, sweet Bion, to thy mouth, and poison thou didst eat . . . And what mortal man so barbarous and wild as to mix it for thee and give it thee at thy call?'[8] – and Shelley, despite the inconsistencies it causes, follows in much the same terms:

> *Our Adonais hath drunk poison – oh!*
> *What deaf and viperous murderer could crown*
> *Life's early cup with such a draught of woe?*
>
> (316–8)

In Bion's poem, Venus laments the death of Adonis killed in the hunt in a speech to which Shelley (though he translated only the beginning of it) was considerably in debt. Adonis is mourned by a host of Fates and Graces, his body ministered to by a group of weeping Loves, all of which Shelley elaborated for the mourning of his Adonais.

But the *Lament for Adonis* is, as we have seen, without consolation, save for the prospect of an annual dirge, and the *Lament for Bion* offers only the idea of an intercession with Proserpina, on the lines of that carried out by Orpheus, which the poet himself seems to admit is fanciful (and which he is too modest to try himself). These models could, then, furnish Shelley with material only for the pathetic side of an elegy. They could offer no explanation which would make sense of the early death of a gifted poet[9] or, indeed, as Shelley required, of mortality in general. Moreover, to one in the habit of creating his own myths, they must finally have seemed remote. The boar (and even the poison) would have been a rather strained indication of Keats's death, which Shelley at that time erroneously believed to have been due to 'the savage criticism on his *Endymion*, which appeared in the *Quarterly Review*' and, he thought, 'produced the most violent effect on his susceptible mind'. This was of particular significance to Shelley since 'One of their associates is, to my knowledge, a most base and unprincipled calumniator' of his own work also. Shelley believed that the poet might be, in Cowper's phrase (of some significance as we shall see) a 'stricken deer', caught in the dilemma of being sincere but unread or actively disliked, or being popular but untrue, and he thought that Keats had been killed because of his great sensitivity in such a role. Thus, to this point at least, Shelley identified himself with Keats, although in fact the two had been acquaintances only of a fairly distant sort. Hence also, the need for consolation. We have, it may seem, a better authenticated case of Milton and King identified in their self-dedication to poetry and seeking assurance that such dedication is worthwhile. But, inasmuch as the cause of death is not an 'accident' but the work of those who 'know not what they do' (Shelley felt so strongly on the matter that, even as a disbeliever, he applied the words of Jesus on Calvary, in *Luke XXIII*) we have also a questioning of things from the point of view of man, the origin and sense of evil in him, and which side of the scale rules triumphant. In all this, Shelley went far beyond anything suggested in his classical sources.

Shelley makes of Keats 'Adonais', which was both metrically convenient (more so than 'Adonis') and suggestive; it suggested the regal and biblical Adonai and also Adonis the victim of the hunt and symbol of death linked with rebirth, the Semitic 'Adon' (lord) being the root of both words. Adonais is the son or adopted son ('nursling') of Urania, 'mighty mother', muse of astronomy, who had been invoked by Milton;[10] Venus Urania was the daughter of Uranus, emerging from the sea after Saturn

59

had thrown his mutilated body there; she is distinct from Venus Aphrodite who loved Adonis, but of course occurred very conveniently as the muse-mother of poetry and of Adonais whom in the other myth her namesake had loved. Thus from Shelley's point of view Urania mourns the death of her latest son and seeks consolation, whilst the myth of Adonis suggests already one form of consolation, namely that represented by seasonal rebirth, the idea of the natural cycle. In practice she does not receive any relief (since it is not suggested that she is an onlooker throughout the poem), and the 'seasonal' consolation is rejected. The actual consolation is produced almost out of a hat in defiance of the fatal reviewer at the turning point of the poem – 'And like a beaten hound tremble thou shalt – as now!' (334) But it is an important part of this solution, stressing its total and transcending quality, that other apparently possible consolations (particularly the seasonal one, which finally returns in a new light, and the idea of a memorial act, which is never quite rejected) should first be reviewed.

The opening of the poem,

> I weep for Adonais – he is dead!
> O weep for Adonais! . . .
> Wake, melancholy Mother, wake and weep! (1–2, 20)

takes its uncompromising assertion of death from Bion, and is close to Shelley's translation:

> I mourn Adonis – loveliest Adonis,
> Dead, dead Adonis – and the Loves lament . . .
> Sleep no more, Venus . . .
> Wake . . . (see note 6)

(Bion's 'loves' become the 'Dreams' of *Adonais* 73ff.) The speaker is not, with an important partial exception, characterised or described. He is not notably part of the pastoral scene, though he observes it. He mentions the review, the 'shaft' which (as we are told at this stage) killed Adonais, and he describes in conventional fashion the absence of Urania at the critical moment: 'Where was lorn Urania When Adonais died?' She was in fact in 'her Paradise' having an audience of an Echo who

> Rekindled all the fading melodies,
> With which, like flowers that mock the corse beneath,
> He had adorned and hid the coming bulk of Death. (16–18)

The 'flowers' are of course Keats's poems, and they operate in a way anticipatory of the 'false surmise' of the floral consolation at the hearse (172ff). They are as Prometheus's hopes,

> *Which sleep within folded Elysian flowers...*
> *That they might hide with thin and rainbow wings*
> *The shape of Death.* (2, iv, 62–4)

But if Venus was in 'her Paradise' when death actually struck, we do not know where she is now. There seems to be no single and consistent setting for the pastoral part of the poem, though it centres around Keat's body in an identified earthly city (Rome, 'that high Capital' – 155), a place where the gathering of the Desires and Adorations, and so forth, with Venus, as well as the clearer procession of mourner poets later on, is not easy to envisage. Again, there is no consistent and dominating tense – we move freely from present, through present-in-the-past, to past and back again, so that the moment of Adonais's death is not clearly defined or related to the lesser happenings. Yet, as Bion's *Lament* centres on the body of Adonis, so Keats's corpse is the focal point of the scenes of mourning in the first part of the poem and, though the mourners are invited to 'Come away' before the body is corrupted by decomposition, are urged, that is, to preserve the illusion of a correspondence between body and spirit, they do not do so. Thus Corruption,

> *The eternal Hunger sits, but pity and awe*
> *Soothe her pale rage, nor dares she to deface*
> *So fair a prey, till darkness and the law*
> *Of change shall o'er his sleep the mortal curtain draw* (69–72),

whilst, in a strange development of Bion's 'Loves', the 'quick Dreams, The passion-winged Ministers of thought', the inspiration of Keats's poetry, attend to the body. He (briefly and not very convincingly) is likened to the shepherd of pastoral, for the 'Dreams' 'were his flocks' which he fed 'near the living streams of his young spirit', and whom he taught 'the love which was its music'.[11] This is of course no mere allusion to Bion, for Shelley argued (notably in the *Defence of Poetry* which also was written in the shadow of Keats's death) that love and poetry were closely related, the one a consummate representation of the other – 'the great instrument of moral good is the imagination, and poetry administers to the effect by acting on the cause', and 'the great secret of morals is love, or a going out of our own nature and an identification of ourselves with the beautiful in a person not our own'. This is a connection which Keats himself repeatedly made.[12] Hence the body of Keats without the Dream or Love is a desolate country, and the Dream a 'Lost Angel of a ruined Paradise' (88), and hence Shelley can translate Bion's Loves, from a myth of the celebration of love itself, into Adonais's ministering Dreams:

> *One from a lucid urn of starry dew*
> *Washed his light limbs as if embalming them;*
> *Another clipped her profuse locks...*

> *Another in her wilful grief would break*
> *Her bow and winged reeds ... (91–7)*

cf. Bion, '*the weeping loves lift up their voices in lamentation; they have shorn their locks for Adonis's sake. This flung upon him arrows, that a bow, this a feather, that a quiver. One hath taken off Adonis's shoe, others fetch water in a golden basin, another washes his thighs.*'[13]

Heavily as Shelley drew on Bion here, and relevant as the myth of Adonis may loosely be, the case of Keats was yet awkwardly different from that of Adonis, for Adonis, if he foolishly ignored the advice of Venus not to hunt, was killed by an accident. The accident may be made to have its implications but obviously it is without any very natural moral. By contrast Adonais (it was one of Shelley's central points) was killed by the circumstance of being a poet, by something reminiscent of Promethean *hubris*. He 'dared to climb' to the highest; therefore he is classed not with those 'their happiness who know', but with 'others more sublime, Struck by the envious wrath of man or god' (38 ff), and in this we perceive again an analogy with the injustice of early death for Lycidas (accidental though that appeared to be despite man's making the 'perfidious bark'); there is as yet no heavenly equivalent to the 'happiness' Adonais ought superlatively to have achieved – 'He will awake no more, oh never more!'

For the moment, although 'sleep', ostensibly a piece of poetic diction but in fact one of the key words in the poem, is insistently present, its implications are not explored, and the classical introductory stage of elegy, the Lamentation, is taken further by reference to the *Lament for Bion*. Recalling the Echo who sang over the 'fading melodies' to Urania, Echo (who fell in love with Narcissus, but was despised by him and pined away)

> *sits among the voiceless mountains*

> *And feeds her grief with his remembered lay,*
> *And will no more reply to wind or fountains...*
> *Since she can mimic not his lips. (128ff)*

cf. 'Moschus', '*Echo too, she mourns among the rocks that she is silent and can imitate your lips no more*'[14]

And, in the classic fashion, Nature is unnatured by death (as occurs at the same point in the *Lament for Bion*):

> *Grief made the young Spring wild, and she threw down*
> *Her kindling buds, as if she Autumn were. (136–7)*

The spring flowers are 'wan and sere', for (140–1) in a somewhat conceited play on the myths of those flowers, Adonis was loved by Hyacinth and Narcissus more than Narcissus (recalling the cause of Echo's death) loved himself, and more than Phoebus loved Hyacinth (who was turned into a flower to commemorate his death by Zephyrus, the rival of Phoebus for his love).

From the conventional mourning of nature Shelley proceeds to develop the first hint of consolation. It is that implicit in the Adonis myth, the knowledge that (whether or not dependent on the ritual worship of the god) the life of spring will replace the death of winter. The hint is destroyed as soon as it is announced since, as the season of Nature is bewildered by the fact of death, so also is the season of the mind. Winter in effect lives on in the sorrower, for the unrelieved cycle is no way out, however merrily nature wakes:

> Ah, woe is me! Winter is come and gone,
> And grief returns with the revolving year. (154–5)

The fiction of the 'young spring' distraught cannot survive; the mourner is alone as Nature is suffused with new life:

> All baser things pant with life's sacred thirst;
> Diffuse themselves; and spend in love's delight,
> The beauty and the joy of their renewed might. (169–71)

But could it be that in this universal process of renewal itself there is a meaningful defeat of death? The body, which in line 69 was awaiting the 'eternal Hunger' of decay to get to work, is now further advanced in corruption, though that too is beautified by new spring:

> The leprous corpse, touched by the spirit tender,
> Exhales itself in flowers of gentle breath;
> Like incarnations of the stars, when splendour
> Is changed to fragrance, they illumine death
> And mock the merry worm that wakes beneath. (172–6)

The disintegration of the body itself breathes life into the flowers, as does the blood of Adonis in Bion's poem. In *Queen Mab* (v, 3–4) death had been seen as 'the imperishable change That renovates the world' and compared with the falling of dead trees which 'fertilise the land they long deformed' so that it produces a new cycle of vegetation. The cycle of nature points to life coming forth out of death, as Hyacinth and Narcissus were themselves immortalised into flowers.

The renewal of physical things is, however, an irrelevance. The endlessly recurring cycle is only pushing the problem back a stage further. Moreover, as is the constant drift of elegists after classical times, man has that within him, whether mind or soul or spirit, which gives him individuality and links him with a world of which this physical cycle can be but a part, if indeed it is a part at all, a world intimately connected with and essentially expressed by love, imagination, poetry (in a sense including the arts). That individuality can with difficulty be believed to survive the process of transformation inherent in the Natural cycle. 'Shall that alone which knows Be as a sword consumed' by invisible lightning? It appears that that which seems peculiarly to merit immortality is alone bereft of it:

> the intense atom glows
> A moment, then is quenched in a most cold repose, (179–80)

and grief itself is of no avail:

> Alas! that all we loved of him should be,
> But for our grief, as if it had not been,
> And grief itself be mortal! Woe is me! (181–3)

In terms of grief these lines are the poem's climax or, for the speaker, its nadir. Finding no consolation in the resurgence of the physical world, he attempts a solution in subjective terms, the survival of what was loved in a kind of frozen love, a grief. And, on the whole, he fails. I say 'on the whole', because the lines are ambiguous and importantly so; they represent a speaker whose mind is not entirely made up. The ambiguity is in tense and syntax. 'That all we loved of him should be . . . as if it had not been' means 'that all we loved of him should not be at all'. But in fact 'our grief' sustains him in a state of non-being, of being as if it had not been. 'Alas!' would make sense alongside a statement that all we loved of him existed no longer, but, in these two lines, the statement is rather the reverse – the disaster is prevented, or at least lessened, by 'our grief'. Then that sophistical hope is itself destroyed by the realisation that 'all we loved of him' (his essential identity) is part of grief, and if the one is mortal the other must be too. And the speaker mingles the hypothetical or conditional with the lament for hard fact; the combination of 'should' with 'that' (rather than with the 'if' which we might expect) continues until the point is settled with 'Woe is me!' The mixed modes and dense, eliptical argument combine to suggest a state of mind, confused and distraught, even obsessive, in face of bereavement.

It is indeed a nice question as to who is speaking here. The 'I' who started by weeping for Adonais and asking where Urania might be is, we presume, one and the same as the 'I' who laments that 'grief returns with the revolving year' (155) and is among the 'we' of the compressed lines on the inability of grief to console. Yet plainly he has in the course of the pastoral (in which his own position is unclear) undergone a new access of feeling, and he associates others, presumably readers, an audience, with his complaint. He now moves from one attempt at consolation to another, until they lead to the inevitable fundamental question and complaint, which is to dominate the second part of the poem in its resolution:

> *Whence are we, and why are we? of what scene*
> *The actors or spectators?*

We are, he concludes at this point, but slaves of a Natural cycle. If there is spirit or soul or love ('that which alone knows'), though subject to that order it makes no sense within that order's terms:

> *Great and mean*
> *Meet massed in death, who lends what life must borrow.*
> *As long as skies are blue, and fields are green,*
> *Evening must usher night, night urge the morrow,*
> *Month follow month with woe, and year wake year to sorrow* (185–9)

It is not until he has come to this conclusion and realised to the full the possible separation of the two worlds of existence, that the speaker can begin to build.

The whole idea of comfort in cyclical death and rebirth is thus abandoned. So also is another ruling concept for the first part of the poem. When the speaker urged the mourners to 'Come away, Haste, while the vault of blue Italian day Is yet his fitting charnel-roof!' (58–60) he continued:

> *He lies, as if in dewy sleep he lay;*
> *Awake him not! surely he takes his fill*
> *Of deep and liquid rest, forgetful of all ill* (61–4)

The body was having 'a mute and uncomplaining sleep' (23). This pretty picture was smeared by the figure of Corruption standing by, which led to the fear that 'He will awake no more, oh never more!', but it was not destroyed and indeed for a short while there appeared to be the very source of spring in 'the leprous corpse' which 'exhales itself in flowers of gentle breath.' Now, however, in a line echoing the other, the notion is more emphatically put – '*He* will awake no more, oh never more!' (190) The essential 'he' as now defined ('all we loved of him') really will 'awake' no more. What consolation there is to be cannot now be a matter of the conventional 'sleep' followed by an 'awakening' in another and superior world, and the essential 'he' will have to be redefined.

With this finality after all the doubt, unconsoling as it plainly is, the speaker, the poet, returns to his pastoral fantasy for the last time, and it centres on Urania. Bion's *Lament for Adonis* also centres on the bereaved Venus, and the two poems have a good deal in common at this stage, save that Urania is the 'mighty mother muse' and Venus a bereaved consort. Thus Bion describes her journey to Adonis (in Shelley's translation) –

> *Aphrodite*
> *With hair unbound is wandering through the woods,*
> *Wild, ungirt, unsandalled – the thorns pierce*
> *Her hastening feet and drink her sacred blood,*[15]

and in *Adonais*,

> *human hearts, which to her aery tread*
> *Yielding not, wounded the invisible*
> *Palms of her tender feet where'er they fell;*
> *And barbed tongues, and thoughts more sharp than they,*
> *Rent the soft form they never could repel,*
> *Whose sacred blood, like the young tears of May,*
> *Paved with eternal flowers that undeserving way.* (210–6)

Plainly, Shelley has taken the opportunity to allegorise the progress of Urania, so that, unlike Aphrodite, she represents the poet suffering (but ultimately winning – 'they never could repel') at the hands of an insensitive world. Then again, whilst Bion has Venus's request for a final kiss, 'but for as long as one short kiss may live' (Shelley's translation), while Venus laments that she is a goddess and cannot accompany him, and while she upbraids him tenderly for going on the fatal hunt (all of which Shelley fairly closely translated), in *Adonais* the whole thing is amended to fit the situation of Adonais as poet and of Urania as chief Muse, who must retain a connection with earth in order to offer inspiration:

> *I would give*
> *All that I now am to be as thou now art!*
> *But I am chained to Time and cannot thence depart!* (232–4)

Moreover, after some unhappy lines comparing the enemies of the poet to those of the hunter (wolves, ravens, vultures), she offers, as Urania is best suited to do (other than the speaker, who has again disappeared) an estimate of the place of the poet in the scheme of things which is the nearest we have yet come to consolation and prepares us for the relative equanimity of the final stage of the 'pastoral' part of the poem, the procession of mourners:

> *The sun comes forth and many reptiles spawn;*
> *He sets, and each ephemeral insect then*
> *Is gathered into death without a dawn,*
> *And the immortal stars awake again;*

66

So is it in the world of living men:
A godlike mind soars forth, in its delight
Making earth bare and veiling heaven, and when
It sinks, the swarms that dimmed or shared its light
Leave to its kindred lamps the spirit's awful night. (253–61)

Here are the sun, as the great poet, reptiles as critics coming to life and then, with night, the stars, true poets temporarily obscured by the brightness of the temporary sun. Adonais is such a 'sun' and evidently, by some undisclosed process, he is to become a 'star', with the 'reptiles' defeated. It is not, perhaps, at this stage a very tangible hope, but its importance is out of proportion to what it actually says, for it presents us with the imagery of light and dark with which the poem will end, and with the 'star' into which Adonais is in fact to be transformed.

The procession of mourners in *Adonais* (262–333) is a sort of bridge-passage. It concludes the pastoral fantasy (the mourners are 'mountain shepherds' from Helicon or Parnassus as Adonais was shepherd of Dreams), as one of the most well-marked elements of that convention (though not in Bion or 'Moschus'). Acting lamentation, constituting tribute, the live symbol of the poem within the poem, it looks back to the mourning speech of Urania and all the solicitousness for the body, and forward to a consolation outside the pastoral world. Thus it represents the position of the speaker who, arrived at a certainty, naked but at least certain, will before long begin to construct, and who, having appeared and disappeared in a none too clear role in the first person hitherto, and having during the long speech of Urania retired well into the wings, now makes a most remarkable appearance – in the third person. In a series of striking and it seems somewhat incongruous images, the 'I' of the poem hitherto, and also its uncharacterised narrator, appears in the procession as 'one frail Form, A Phantom among men', comes also as a representative of Dionysus or Bacchus, god of wine but symbolic also of passionate poetry, complete with the light 'thyrsus' spear and crown of ivy which accompanied Dionysus.

There are reasons, of course, for this surprising personage here in the poem. He is part of the same conception of poetry by which we have seen Urania afflicted, with her feet wounded by hardened hearts and barbed tongues tearing at her body, of the Promethean view associated earlier with Adonais and particularly, of course, with the myth of Adonis the hunter who is slain in the hunt. Now he is an Actaeon (who was turned into a stag, for watching Diana bathing, and devoured by his own dogs):

he, as I guess,
Had gazed on Nature's naked loveliness,

67

Actaeon-like, and now he fled astray
With feeble steps o'er the world's wilderness,
And his own thoughts, along that rugged way,
Pursued, like raging hounds, their father and their prey. (274–9)

This recalls perhaps Cowper, the 'stricken deer' (*The Garden* 108):

> *He came the last, neglected and apart;*
> *A herd-abandoned deer struck by the hunter's dart.*

But while he is something of a type, the embodiment of a conception not unusual (that exceptional merits turn on their owner, whether or not because they correspond to some other deficiency), he is not merely that. As a mourner he shows exceptional decrepitude, but also exceptional grief for personal loss.[16] He is 'a Love in desolation masked' (281), 'companionless as the last cloud of an expiring storm' (273), a 'withering flower' on which 'the killing sun smiles brightly', whose cheek can burn with blood 'even while the heart may break' (288). He has a 'branded and ensanguined brow' like those brows of Cain and Christ, celebrated outcasts. He speaks in the 'accents of an unknown land', not because he is an Englishman in Rome, as are the other mourners, but presumably because his language of poetry is misunderstood. For this is neither 'I' (another 'I' is even now telling of him – 'as I guess'), nor Shelley (a young man of 28 and in good health, though certainly feeling misunderstood), nor an entirely imaginary being. It is, in fact, a mixture of all three.

Perhaps no reader can find all this entirely satisfactory, since the various aspects tend to conflict with each other. As a picture of Shelley it is implausible and implies a gross and nauseating self-pity for which no justification is given. As a picture of the main 'I' speaker or narrator it might have been better suggested at the beginning and then woven into the whole with some consistency instead of being an isolated portrait. As a sketch of an entirely imaginary being it has too many details which suggest the other 'real' elements. But, in sum, I suppose, the objection is that it is an exaggeration; pity for the self is a normal associate of grief for another, but hardly to this extent. It is embarrassing for one who is confessedly 'apart', in a symbolic way, to receive such prominence. It might have been well if the passage on 'Whence are we, and why are we?' had been manifestly the utterance of a character in the poem who had been seen to arrive at such a pass, but in fact these reflective lines, and the two or three other short passages like them were as interpolations (although in fact summings up) into the fresco of echoes and dreams and washing light limbs with starry dew.

Yet I do not think it can be doubted that exaggeration of a sort is the point of the section. We have here what is virtually a caricature of grief, when unrelieved grief is the state in which the speaker was last seen. The awkwardness arises because, whilst the caricature makes good sense in terms of what is to come, it does not make clear sense of what has already been. Moreover, it is not thorough-going and consistent caricature. There is a great difference between the fellow whose 'ever-beating heart' caused the thyrsus to shake in his 'weak hand' (a feature of the passage is its profligacy of 'weak' epithets – dying, falling, killing, feeble, expiring, and so on), and the Actaeon image of the poet as father of the thoughts which hunt him. We do not doubt, because it is related to other images in the poem and to the Adonis myth as a whole, that the latter is a concept meant in all seriousness – the 'deer' stricken by the 'dart' is plainly of a type with Adonais 'pierced by the shaft' (11) and this is another instance of the identification of the mourner and the mourned.

In consequence of this inconsistency in the fantasy, the boundaries of the caricature are perilously uncertain; it is one thing for the mourner to 'distance' himself by the portrayal of an excessive grief in terms of a consolation yet to come, but it is another for us to react with a feeling of the ridiculous because the figure does not make sense in terms of what we have been shown. It is well and true that the poet and the speaker are identified as one 'Who in another's fate now wept his own' (300). That is credible of the process of grief and a fundamental part of the tradition, as we have seen. But what are we to make of the fact that 'all stood aloof' (for he is an outcast) and 'smiled through their tears' at the unintelligible language of his mourning, and why should Urania mock the reader's intelligence by 'murmuring' 'Who art thou?', when the other mourners (Byron and Moore, who seem to receive tribute as political rebels rather than as having revered Keats, and Hunt who is more plausible) apparently pose no problem but for the reader are a good deal less distinct? We may conclude, I think, that there is an element of exaggeration in the passage which is designed to reveal itself at the time of consolation, but that the portrayal was in any case too big a risk to take and the poet almost certainly let in a little of his own self-pity once he had agreed to give himself such an opportunity.

Before the speaker made his first venture into consolation (by way of the seasons) he launched a curse on the reviewer who killed Adonais, a curse significantly worded in view of his comparison of himself later to Cain:

the curse of Cain

Light on his head who pierced thy innocent breast,
And scared the angel soul that was its earthly guest! (151–3)

So now, about to begin the second, consolatory, part of the poem, he again vents his feelings in a parallel sentiment (save that, following Bion, he now attributes the death within the pastoral to poison[17] rather than to an arrow):

> *Live thou, whose infamy is not thy fame!*
> *Live! fear no heavier chastisement from me,*
> *Thou noteless blot on a remembered name!*
> *But be thyself, and know thyself to be!*
> *To spill the venom when thy fangs o'erflow:*
> *Remorse and self-contempt shall cling to thee;*
> *How shame shall burn thy secret brow,*
> *And like a beaten hound tremble thou shalt – as now.* (325–33)

The recurrence of the curse is interesting because it portends the leaving (here the final leaving) of the Adonis-scene. It suggests that, despite the uncertainty of person, despite the third-person portrayal of 'Shelley', and despite the binary form of the poem with two nearly self-contained sections, there is a moving mind, the rudimentary depiction of the progress of the real spokesman-mourner of the poem, behind the work.

What the curses represent is the intrusion of (what Shelley believed to be) the events of the real world. Thus they correspond to those sections of *Lycidas* beginning 'Ay me!' and which show, bursting into the idea that the nymphs might have saved Lycidas or that the tribute of flowers is possible as expressive tribute, the reality that the seas and shores are washing him far away. These are the events before which the 'pastoral' is of no avail. And so also it is with *Adonais*. The unity with Nature does not assuage grief – 'Ah woe is me! . . . grief returns with the revolving year.' But as the speaker of *Lycidas* proceeds, when his grief appears least consolable, to a reversing act of faith, so does the speaker of *Adonais* – an effect made more dramatic (too dramatic, for some) by that final 'as now', which is suggestive of the conjuror producing his final trick, or the well-placed clue to the next instalment of a serial fiction.

'Sleep' is the starting point of the final phase. When no immortality was found in grief, the speaker declared, '*He* will awake no more, oh, never more!', thinking of earthly life but also in terms of another world, virtually unreal because so remote, as the Christian afterlife may appear. But now, first there is an element of doubt in the whole analogy ('He wakes or sleeps with the enduring dead' (336) – it does not seem to matter which), and then:

> *Peace, peace! he is not dead, he doth not sleep –*
> *He hath awakened from the dream of life.* (343–4)

The speaker addresses either himself or the reader (there has always been presumed identity between them except in the 'mourner' passage),

70

apostrophising them for their slowness in realising what, in truth, he is presented as having only just realised himself. It is an abandonment of the idea of a life of wakefulness followed by a death of sleep[18], in favour of the idea of a life which is a 'dream' compared with the real life to which one awakens on death, this real life being in a particular relationship to the 'dream'. Thus the 'sleep' image is turned upside down; when one dies, one does not go to sleep, an image suggesting some future awakening and associated with a concept of purgatory, but one wakes up. Once that is established, we move on from the image of 'sleep' to the image of life as a 'veil', which hides or sets up a haze before the true reality. Life is bounded, in the upward vision, by the 'dome' of the sky beyond which, if we could see through it (the idea is figurative) we should again perceive unlimited truth. These images have, of course, been prepared for in the poem, in, for example, the suggestion that Adonais be not awakened 'while still He lies, as if in dewy sleep he lay' (60–1) and 'while the vault of blue Italian day' is still a fit 'roof' for the undecayed body. But this is not to say that we at all expect their development, and an effect of sudden inversion, almost of ecstatic discovery, given whatever structural problems it may pose.

Such are the themes with which the consolation of *Adonais* is concerned. Though here they achieve some of their finest expressions, they are not peculiar to this poem. In *Mont Blanc* (1816), for instance, Shelley explores the two ideas of sleep, tending first to contrast a 'slumber' of death with a wakefulness of life, but moving on to speculate that in his intense spiritual awareness he is himself 'in dream', coming very near to the idea that the true wakefulness is the 'dream', what is seen behind 'The veil of life and death':

> Some say that gleams of a remoter world
> Visit the soul in sleep, – that death is slumber . . . (49–50)

He looks up at Mont Blanc, 'far, far above, piercing the infinite sky', and asks,

> Has some unknown Omnipotence unfurled
> The veil of life and death? Or do I lie
> In dream, and does the mightier world of sleep
> Spread far around and inaccessibly
> Its circles? (49–57)

The mountain appears to pierce through the dome ('the infinite dome of heaven' – 140) which bounds earthly reality, or, in another parallel and very beautiful image, the mountain's coloured surface is as a rainbow stretching across the screen of foam over a waterfall, behind which is beauty and reality not yet shaped into earthly form:

> *Thine earthly shadows stretched across the sweep*
> *Of the etherial waterfall, whose veil*
> *Robes some unsculptured image ... (27–9)*

Shelley does not use the comparison with entire consistency, but in general, when used in this connection the 'veil' is the boundary between life and death (death and life). The veil is something to pass through, something akin to the act or process of dying. Alternatively, the corresponding reality of earth is a 'stain', something which obscures. Thus, in *Adonais* (356) 'From the contagion of the world's slow stain He is secure' or, earlier, the Dream which ministered to the body, unaffected by earth, 'as with no stain she faded' (89). Again, 'the veil of daylight' may be mortal life, as in *The Sensitive Plant* (20). In two of the most celebrated lines of *Adonais*, the 'veil' image and the image of the mist are united so that death or dying is a sort of semi-transparent material which covers but does not obscure the reality between which and earthly life it falls:

> *Death is a low mist which cannot blot*
> *The brightness it may veil.* (391–2)

Elsewhere, earthly life is the curtain covering real life which is known only in death, 'the painted veil, by those who were, called life', a 'loathesome mask' to be torn aside, 'the veil which those who live call life',[19] and, in a sonnet, 'Lift not the painted veil which those who live Call life', where life 'mimics' reality with but partial colours. In such images we are plainly concerned with an inversion dependent on viewpoint; those who live call it 'life', but those who have gone further call it the 'painted veil', just as for those who live life may be wakefulness and for the dead it may be 'sleep' or 'dream'. The difference corresponds to the difference between the first and second parts of *Adonais*; the reader is expected to look at things the other way round in the second part, and it is a question whether he has been sufficiently prompted to make the adjustment (though his scepticism will be rather for the first part in retrospection than for the consolation).

These images of all meet in the peroration of *Adonais* (460–4), where the symbols of 'dome', 'veil' and 'stain' are fused into a picture of stained glass in a dome beyond which is the One, the Truth, as the Heaven is conventionally beyond the 'azure sky' (of Rome; recalling the 'blue vault of the Italian day' in 1.60), and the veil is shattered by the death so that the Absolute becomes truly visible:

> *The One remains, the many change and pass;*
> *Heaven's light forever shines, Earth's shadows fly;*

> *Life, like a dome of many-coloured glass,*
> *Stains the white radiance of Eternity,*
> *Until death tramples it to fragments.*

Of this lesser life, mourning Nature, the 'caverns and forests', 'faint flowers and fountains' (for Shelley seems to allude back to the pastoral convention of Nature mourning) is a part. The mourning is itself partial untruth, an obscuring 'stain', a 'scarf' thrown on the earth to obscure its truth, or a 'mourning veil' (367). The concept of this Truth is not of a remote and unconnected One, but of an essence interpenetrating though unhappily obscured. *Adonais* is 'made one with Nature' (370), not as the body rotted to be reborn in the cycle (the consolation rejected previously – lines 172–3), but as the 'presence' of the essential Power which moves Nature; he is 'withdrawn' by that Power 'to its own' (376–7), only to re-enter the world in true being;

> *He is a presence to be felt and known*
> *In darkness and in light, from herb and stone,*
> *Spreading itself where'er that Power may move*
> *Which has withdrawn its being to his own;*
> *Which wields the world with never-wearied love,*
> *Sustains it from beneath, and kindles it above.* (373–8)

This is a spirit shaping chaotic and stubborn material, Platonic essence 'informing' matter:

> *He is a portion of the loveliness*
> *Which he made more lovely; he doth bear*
> *His part, while the one Spirit's plastic stress*
> *Sweeps through the dull dense world, compelling there,*
> *All new successions to the forms they wear;*
> *Torturing th'unwilling dross that checks its flight*
> *To its own likeness ...* (379–85)

But in practice, of course, these are images within a continuity, and this second part of *Adonais* is characterised by a gathering movement to the ultimate statement of the relations, not of Adonais to the One or to Nature, but of the speaker's relationship to Adonais; the definition of the existence of Adonais, which is also the tribute to him, is, if not the lesser thing, at least for the purposes of the poem a stage in the finding of consolation for the speaker rather than for Adonais himself. This consolation arises from the concept of a power which is transcendent (he is pictured as 'soaring' and 'outsoaring' beyond our ken, beyond 'the shadow of the night', and as being literally 'secure', without care), but also immanent, 'made one with Nature', 'a presence to be felt and known In darkness and in light'. The conception is neo-Platonic, but it is of a Platonism wherein the lower

73

stages are purified and growing towards the higher and death is a sort of short cut. Thus, in an image of growing importance throughout the poem, recalling Urania's likeness of the newly famous to the sun and of the established eminences to the stars (253–6), the ascent of the heavenly bodies, seemingly from the earth to the summit of the 'dome' of sky, indicates not transcendent coldness, but a continuity, masked only by the 'veil' between the world of time and the timeless:

> *The splendours of the firmament of time*
> *May be eclipsed, but are extinguished not;*
> *Like stars to their appointed height they climb ...* (388–90)

Comparably, the 'inheritors of unfulfilled renown' built thrones which begin in the earthly context, but are completed, fulfilled, in the Unapparent; Adonais is to join the age's symbol of unfulfilment (Chatterton, the 'boy poet' who committed suicide at the age of eighteen), and the to us perhaps more convincing exemplars, Sidney[20] and Lucan[21]. These 'and many more' welcome Keats among them 'as one of us', 'robed in dazzling immortality' in the manner of a Christian apotheosis, and admitting him as the 'Vesper' (the favourite pastoral evening-star) 'of our throng' (406ff). So he 'is gathered to the kings of thought'.

As if to remind us of the distance travelled since the opening pastoral ministrations to the body, the grave in Rome is visited in the imagination, recalling the building of the monument and the strewing of the bier which are so common in the convention. But, although it is made, as the flowers of *Lycidas*'s 'false surmise' are all but gathered, the tribute is a ritual only, for the real 'he' is elsewhere, and this is the sepulchre 'Oh, not of him, but of our joy' (425. One notes again the assumption of a crucial definition of 'he'). It is, despite its beauty ('A light of laughing flowers along the grass is spread' as in the convention) and its reminder of memorials ('one keen pyramid with wedge sublime' 444[22]), perhaps almost because of these things, an irrelevance and an escape:

> *From the world's bitter wind*
> *Seek shelter in the shadow of a tomb.*
> *What Adonais is, why fear we to become?*

We are urged, then, (for the speaker has addressed himself to those who still mourn, the 'fond wretches' who still clasp with their souls mere 'Earth' (415–6), and these are, for rhetorical purposes, all his readers), to take a step of faith before which the expected reaction is 'fear'. The coda persuades us to take on a belief in the light of which

> *Rome's azure sky,*
> *Flowers, ruins, statues, music, words, are weak.* (466–7)

74

Then, so personal is this reorientation, that the plural audience becomes a singular one, and the speaker exhorts himself to accept the vision of the united concepts and images of transcendence and immanence, by the mystery of which ('Love') every created thing and being is a 'mirror' of 'the fire for which all thirst'. Yet, even as he does so, the speaker is struck by the magnitude of the undertaking, and he agrees 'darkly', 'fearfully'.

The final lines bring to a climax the images of Adonais as a star and of life as a veil over ultimate reality. They incorporate also allusions and parallels to related poems. The soul is in a 'bark'[23], like the boat of Henry King's *Exequy*, and the movement steady towards an equally remote yet certain destination. Guided by the 'beacon' of the star, it is under the influence of a benign power, such as the 'genius of the shore' in *Lycidas*, for 'the dead live there' and influence the heart impelled by 'lofty thought' (392–6). Going 'far from the trembling throng', recalling Gray's 'madding crowd', at once suggests something somewhat patrician in the whole concept and implies purposeful movement away from the aimless drifting of a society. The role of outcast, the Cain- or Christ-figure, is now deliberately chosen (or is seen to have purpose) rather than being the result of victimisation. He is, in the final tribute, inspired by the 'breath' of the lost poet he has invoked, and the breath may perhaps also suggest that breeze which so persistently accompanies the numinous experiences of poets:

> *The breath whose might I have invoked in song*
> *Descends on me; my spirit's bark is driven,*
> *Far from the shore, far from the trembling throng*
> *Whose sails were never to the tempest given;*
> *The massy earth and sphered skies are riven!*
> *I am borne darkly, fearfully afar;*
> *Whilst, burning through the inmost veil of Heaven,*
> *The soul of Adonais, like a star,*
> *Beacons from the abode where the Eternal are.*

It might perhaps be wondered whether in *Adonais* Shelley was not perhaps in a secondary way 'Actaeon-like' – both 'father' and 'prey' to his own thoughts. He referred to poetry by means of that favourite Romantic symbol, the Aeolian lyre, in which the soul or heart of the poet is as the lyre whose strings are set vibrating by the wind of inspiration;

> *Man is an instrument over which a series of external and internal impressions are driven, like the alternations of an ever-changing wind over an Aeolian lyre, which move it by their motion to ever-changing melody.*

So he wrote near the beginning of the *Defence of Poetry*. But man, he affirmed, produces not simple melody, but also harmony, 'an internal adjustment of the sounds or motions thus excited to the impressions which excite them'. The nature of this 'adjustment', and in particular to what extent it is under the control of the conscious will and its success or failure is reflected in the success or failure of a poem, Shelley does not define. It may be that Shelley in his theory gave less than due to the organising and craftsmanly aspects of art and that the deficiency is apparent in the structure of *Adonais*. In terms of the 'harp' the fictionalised situation may correspond to that produced from outside, the 'melody', and the second part of the poem may correspond to the uncertainly related 'harmony', or vice versa. Yet, as has been said, there is evidence that he considered the poem more than customarily highly-wrought, and it is also true that the elegiac convention specialises in the paradox of artful artlessness, the suggestion of equivocations and uncertainties of expression which are dramatically plausible as corresponding to the manner of a distraught mourner.

There are signs of an overriding 'dramatic' structure at work in *Adonais*, but I do not think that it succeeds in governing the poem's effect. There is also another pattern, the binary form in which pastoral is simply superseded by what we may shortly call 'Platonic', and one assumes that there is more to this supersession than that the poet changed his mind in mid-course. But finally, the problem is that neither of these forms satisfactorily controls the poem as a whole and, perhaps worse, that they tend to conflict with each other.

On either basis, there is a marked change shortly after the uneasy portrayal of Shelley as a 'phantom among men', one of the mourners. This portrayal, it has already been suggested, has elements of caricature and exaggeration in it, and it is the emphatic and total nature of the consolation towards the poem's end which shows us the reason for these elements; this extreme mourner within the procession, within the 'pastoral', represents the mistaken mourner, the 'fond wretch' who persists in the delusion that 'him', the essence of Adonais, is identical with 'our joy', now exposed as an irrelevance and therefore ridiculous as an object of mourning. He takes 'He' in '*He* will awake no more' as being the essential rather than the contingent Adonais, whereas that this 'He' will awake no more is later shown to be neither here nor there. Thus Shelley the artist, we might say, has overplanned; he knew of the consolation that was to come, and of its nature, and he let that knowledge affect the 'pastoral' before it was reasonable, from the reader's point of view, to do so.

But, if we look at it from the 'dramatic' point of view throughout, rather than as a pastoral followed by a consolation which, both in content and as a convention, supersedes the pastoral, we find that there are the intrusions of reality in which 'I' takes the pastoral very much more seriously, making it the basis of the discussion of consolation by analogy with the seasonal cycle. We are then obliged to see the final consolation as a culmination of an internal discussion, in the context of which the comparative weakness and over-decorative nature of the pastoral may be justified as the expressions of a mind at odds with itself. But in that case, since we last saw the first-person speaker in despair ('Whence are we, and why are we?' 184), are we not obliged to take the portrayal of the mourner as a direct representation of such a state of mind, an interpretation which the details and tone of the description scarcely permit us to make? And is it, or is it not, to any purpose that 'I' backs out of the poem in its middle section so that Urania, for her big speech, is introduced as 'she' instead of the 'thou' of personal address used hitherto?

I think that the poem is better read from the 'dramatic' point of view, despite the difficulties, and that we are for the most part to identify with 'I' and the narrator. This can only be done if he is viewed tentatively as the artist consciously considering the pastoral mode of expression and trying to find consolation within it. Finally, being unable to do so, he abandons pastoral and the Adonis story. At the same time, certain aspects of the Adonis myth (most notably what it is taken to say of the plight and status of the artist) are assumed not to be rejected; for it has to be recognised that, total as is the nature of the final consolation, it reinforces rather than diminishes the notion of the artist's isolation ('far from the shore, far from the trembling throng') which, largely seen, is the cause of the death of Adonais. Whilst the conclusion may give purpose and even justification to set out on such a voyage, it does nothing to lessen the problems over and above grief to which the speaker, when presented as mourner, seems to require solution.

This 'dramatic' reading involves more identification of the speaker and poet, both addressing the reader in terms fairly direct, and more emphasis on the mind to be salved, than does the conception of the 'poet-figure' in Gray's *Elegy* or the 'uncouth swain' in *Lycidas*. We know very little of the narrator as a person except what is shown in the 'distanced' description of the mourner in the procession, which it is hard indeed to take at its face value. The bowing-out of the narrator (that is, of the first person) in the middle of the poem is associated with the effort to present him from outside in the 'mourner' passage; they are part and parcel of a new attempt to adjust to the situation, through the ritual procession. The device is, of course, shattered by the intrusion of the self-pity into the mourner's character and then by the violence of the curse which follows. But for an uncertain period the speaker's misery has been in part a performance, an act, in the knowledge of a consolation coming, and that is why the curse can be concluded '. . . as now' (333). It is the consolation which will be the source of the 'shame' and 'trembling' which have been wished on the reviewer, and the consolation will also achieve a more stable relationship of

77

speaker, 'poet', and reader, in which poet and speaker are virtually indistinguishable.

If such a reading poses problems, it does, I think, avoid the greater danger of the alternative, in which consolation and pastoral are static opposed and contrasted sections of equal artistic value yet where, it seems plain, the larger 'pastoral' part offers principally the title, and the consolation offers the value. 'The parts of a composition', Shelley wrote in the *Defence of Poetry*, 'may be poetical, without the composition as a whole being a poem.' *Adonais* is, surely, imperfect as a complete work of art. Yet we do feel that we are talking of a poem.

V

Arnold – *The Scholar-Gipsy* and *Thyrsis*

With Arnold's two related elegies we encounter fully an aspect of the tradition which we might regard as released by the Romantic Poets, characteristic in various ways of the Victorians, and indeed continuous to our own times. I mean, of course, a way of looking at the countryside which, beside Sicily and Arcady, especially when nearly fossilised in the Renaissance convention, seems comparatively realistic, based on specific observation. We are considering not the groves of Pan with nymphs and naiads, with Echo and a selection of flowers approved for their mythological ancestry, nor even with Christ and angels who may appear or stand not far in the background, but rather the Oxford countryside as, from a rather select viewpoint, it could reasonably be observed.

Yet the difference is not absolute nor the change sudden. We have seen how Johnson would prefer, to Milton's shepherds driving a field and battening their flocks, Cowley's description of himself and Hervey at Cambridge (where, however, the personification of 'fields' and 'ye gentle trees', let alone the suggestion that they fade when told to, will strike us as a kinship with the fossils). We have noted also the description (highly selective though in no adverse sense) of Gray's evening in the churchyard, written by one who confessedly played down natural description in his verse. So it is apparent, without citing a long list of examples, that whilst the less selective and infinitely more varied descriptions by Wordsworth – himself following on and adopting conventions of the 'topographical' poets, and of Goldsmith, Thomson, and Akenside – beyond doubt had a liberating influence, they inaugurated no sudden change so far as elegy is concerned.

Secondly, not only was there no sudden change but, so far as this way of looking is concerned, the change itself is but one of degree, in that the 'nature' of Arnold is itself an artifice, a construction. What we are concerned with is not the substitution of the real for the ideal, but the substitution of one ideal (to some extent a personal and individual one) for another. Arnold opposes, within an overall context of 'natural' themes and imagery, the countryside of his imagination to the world around him, the world in which he is aware of a sense of loss. His description is based particularly on the recalled moment and its recollected setting, and he is apt, as is any elegist, to present what is lost in an attractive light which is a substitute for the honeyed joys of Arcady. What is new is the very great development of the short passages (as *Lycidas*, lines 23–36, Gray's *Elegy* 97–114) which recite the situation before the loss. To achieve the definition of the loss becomes of vital importance. There is a suggestion of compulsiveness about the way the details are set down. A large proportion of these poems of Arnold is devoted to this sort of description. It is as if the detailed re-creation, the successful embodiment, of the lost world will in some way of itself confer upon it an immortality, a capability to transcend time, even if it cannot be directly restored.

Correspondingly, when we witness the conventional 'return' of the speaker to the situation surrounding the poem, it is not, in *Thyrsis*, to a 'pastoral' world outside his reflections that he returns (as does Milton's 'swain' considering what 'tomorrow' holds) but to a world opposed to 'natural' or 'pastoral', and which he has somehow to reconcile with it. The speaker returns to what is fairly plainly life contemporary with the poet. We have seen in *Adonais* the unstable but finally asserted identity of the speaker with the 'poet'. In *Thyrsis* the identity is both more stable and more complete. The poem is declared to be a 'monody', and it is plain from the prefatory note ('to commemorate the author's friend, Arthur Hugh Clough, who died at Florence, 1861') that it is conceived in relation to *Lycidas* ('In this monody the author bewails a learned friend . . .'). But there is the very great difference that, apart from a few equivalences of pipes and poems and references to 'swains', it is not the monody of a Sicilian shepherd. Indeed, there is very little of the 'disguise' (to which Johnson so strongly objected) in Arnold's poem. The speaker refers to Sicilian pastoral as to a thing in the past whose conventional resorts in face of grief are largely irrelevant to his problem. The deliberate 'distancing', the imaginary world of which the speaker during his monody is conventionally a part, and on which the poet as distinct from the speaker makes his own final comment – these are scarcely present.

The distinction between lyrical meditations such as Keats's *Odes*, by which Arnold was deeply influenced (and whose stanza form he imitates), and monody or dramatic monologue would appear to lie in the variety of detail given in the work to support and explain the motivation of the speaker, over and above any direct comment from a narrator. If we realise that our knowledge of the speaker is greater than his of himself, we conclude that we have a manipulated spokesman, dramatic rather than lyrical conception. Of material evidencing such a distinction as this, Arnold's poetry (perhaps most crucially in the would-be drama, *Empedocles on Etna*) has very little. That is not to say that the poet-figure *is* Arnold, nor to say that if he gets his facts wrong (as, in *Thyrsis*, in the interests of his poetic intention, he does) the poem must fail and Arnold be upbraided for falsification. But it is to say that this is a 'monody' with a design upon us, that it is nearer the lyrical than the dramatic. It is not monody multi-faceted and offered for contemplation as 'invention' with a life of its own, but, though undoubtedly a work of art, the expression of sentiments seeking identification rather than a sceptical or ironic scrutiny. In the case of *Adonais* there is, as we have seen, considerable doubt on this score, but in the case of *The Scholar-Gipsy* and *Thyrsis* there is very little.

The Scholar-Gipsy is a nearly essential prelude to *Thyrsis*, as Arnold himself stated in his *New Poems* volume of 1867 – 'throughout this poem there is reference to another piece, *The Scholar-Gipsy*'. It is interesting from a formal point of view that Arnold had not called this 'other piece' a 'monody' as well, and did not incorporate into it more classical material. One has the feeling that the form of the one had a good deal to do with the form of the other and that at a certain stage in the composition of *Thyrsis* Arnold, realising that he had previously written something approaching pastoral elegy, decided to bring the new poem more obviously into line with the convention. For, in the broadest sense, *The Scholar-Gipsy* is both elegy and pastoral, although it is not an elegy purportedly concerned to lament the death and unfulfilment of a friend. As a pastoral, it compares not two worlds, but three; it relates an idyllic Oxford country in the past (the poem was written in about 1853[1] and centres on scenes recalled from eight or more years earlier), the Seventeenth Century of Glanvill's originating story, and the present world viewed with deep disenchantment.

The opening (but only the opening) is pastoral in the old allegorical manner. It gives a remoteness, an interior quality, to the whole which is indeed part of the theme. The speaker is with a 'shepherd' whom he sends off, in a rhetorical fashion (an opening, as it were, *in medias res*), to attend to the sheep – 'Go, for they call you, shepherd, from the hill!' – while he himself finds a quiet 'nook o'er the high, half-reaped field' to read and reflect in 'the live murmur of a summer's day' (20). This speaker is not referred to as a shepherd himself. It appears that the shepherd, as one with the daily task of feeding the sheep, may represent some regularly employed teacher,[2] and this would of course be Clough, who had a Fellowship at Oriel College whilst Arnold was an undergraduate, although by the time Arnold read Glanvill's *Vanity of Dogmatizing*, with its account of the Scholar-Gipsy, in 1845, Clough and Arnold were both Fellows at Oriel. The students, if this is the allusion, are described in terms recalling 'the hungry sheep look on and are not fed' of *Lycidas*, line 125 ('No longer leave thy wistful flock unfed' – (3)), and the whole opening fancy reminds us of Milton's description of the association of his speaker and Lycidas before their separation. With this 'shepherd', the speaker of *The Scholar-Gipsy* is engaged in a 'joint quest', which is not at present described, and it is arranged that the two will meet up again in the quiet moonlight when the day's work is done, and 'again begin the quest' (10); Thyrsis and the speaker are engaged 'on like quest' in *Thyrsis* (211). In point of fact the poem never returns to the setting or the assignation, since the speaker is overtaken by a stream of reflection which forms the substance of the work and from which we do not see him emerge, although this reflection itself certainly tends towards a definition of the 'quest'. The shepherd is not portrayed as the shepherd of flocks of thoughts (that is, as a poet) as in *Adonais* and the speaker is not portrayed as a shepherd at all. The opening literal 'pastoral' seems designed entirely to set the poem as a whole into the convention.

Once the setting is established and the speaker has 'read the oft-read tale again' of the Scholar who, 'tired of knocking at preferment's door', forsook his friends to join the gipsies and learn a secret art of mesmerism (a fashionable interest which was at one stage to have bulked larger in the poem), the speaker is led rapidly into characterisation of the Scholar and to the feeling that he has himself seen him. The Scholar-Gipsy is 'pensive and tongue-tied', and in the face of company 'he would fly'. He is seen only in 'rare glimpses' – glimpses to be recounted until the turning point of the poem – in a manner similar to and with a character as fleeting and enigmatic as that of the 'youth' whom the 'hoary-headed swain' of Gray's *Elegy* cannot fathom.

But only two such glimpses are mentioned in a general way before the narration undergoes a startling change. Hitherto, the speaker has been paraphrasing Glanvill's book, and describing the past encounters of others. Now, in the middle of a stanza he starts to address the Scholar-Gipsy directly as 'thou', and his tense becomes of the present or the immediate past:

> But, mid their drink and clatter, he would fly.
> And I myself seem half to know thy looks ... (61–2)

He continues to address him as an intimate, an intimacy made to sound privileged, and presuming an identity of the Scholar-Gipsy and himself by the nature of the epithets and phrases in which the spirit is described and which are applied equally to the places which he haunts, 'For most, I know, thou lov'st retiréd ground' – 'lone wheatfields', 'shy retreats', 'quiet place', 'shy fields', and so on. Typical scenes of the country round Oxford are recalled and with each the Scholar-Gipsy is associated through the seasons and in his own quietist way. In summer he is trailing his fingers in the stream until the ferry unloads its passengers; and then 'thou art seen no more'. Girls have met him whilst on the way to a May Day dance and have received beautiful flowers from him; but they have never heard him speak. In June he has been seen by bathers on their way to a millpond; but when they return, he has gone. In autumn, the blackbird has watched him fearlessly, for he was 'rapt', the melancholy man awaiting inspiration, 'waiting for the spark from heaven to fall' (120). 'And once, in winter' – the only direct encounter mentioned – the speaker himself has met him and watched him climb to Cumnor Hill to look down through the snow at 'the line of festal light in Christ Church hall.'

These are the accounts and the memories which reading Glanvill stirs. By a combination of personal and scenic description they have given us the essentials of what the Scholar-Gipsy represents – a claim, at least, to esoteric wisdom, the fugitive habits and placid brooding, as also the generosity of the voluntary outsider who is sustained by an inner conviction and is at odds neither with himself nor with men at large (from whom, however, he shies). But the Scholar-Gipsy is of course more than that. He is also the scenery which shares his attributes; the two are interwoven so that this aspect of the country, which for the speaker exists in memory, is itself a value. It is no more than sketched, but this, which exists in conflict with another world in which he is increasingly immersed, an ideal which is threatened not only for the speaker but in its very existence by that other world, represents one form of modern pastoral, one partial and idealised view of existence compared with another:

> At some lone homestead in the Cumnor hills,
> Where at her open door the housewife darns,
> Thou hast been seen, or hanging on a gate
> ' To watch the threshers in the mossy barns.
> Children, who early range these slopes and late
> For cresses from the rills,
> Have known thee eying, all an April-day,
> The springing pastures and the feeding kine;
> And marked thee, when the stars come out and shine,
> Through the long dewy grass move slow away. (101–10)

It is a view of domestic and agricultural peace, 'lone' (away, as the Scholar-Gipsy always is, from the 'madding crowd'), representing regular, purposeful work, but also the children playing, among the placid but lively 'springing pastures and the feeding kine'. It is not mere 'nature

83

description', but on the other hand, plainly it omits an uncomfortable side of such a community which must be equally real and conditioned by the same unspecified factors. We cannot say that the ideal represented by the Scholar-Gipsy is false; but it requires a considerable act of faith to believe that it may be valid.

It is with that act of faith that the second part of *The Scholar-Gipsy* is concerned. Still, so far as we know, screened in his 'nook', and not (again, as far as we know) prompted by any external event, the speaker is suddenly struck by the distance his thought has taken him, the distance of his vision from reality, in particular insofar as it embodies as an essential element the person of the Scholar-Gipsy (whom he still addresses). The realisation is akin to those of *Lycidas* ('Ay me! I fondly dream' – 56, and 'Ay me! Whilst thee the shores and sounding seas...' – 154) or *Adonais* ('Ah, woe is me! Winter is come and gone...' – 154); it is related also to the similar awakenings after apostrophe in Keats's *Odes*:

> But what – I dream! Two hundred years are flown
> Since first thy story ran through Oxford halls. (131–2)

For, in this temporal reality, the Scholar is dead and lying in a graveyard which bears a distinct resemblance to that of the 'youth' in Gray's *Elegy*:[3]

> And thou from earth art gone
> Long since, and in some quiet churchyard laid –
> Some country-nook, where o'er thy unknown grave
> Tall grasses and white flowering nettles wave,
> Under a dark, red-fruited yew-tree's shade. (136–40)

This stanza (131–40), in which the reality of the previous 'dream' is suddenly questioned, is the pivot of the poem and it represents something of an inversion of normal elegiac processes of thought. For here there is subjected to analysis the subjective assurance of an immortality which seems never to be in doubt. The incredulity of 'But what – I dream!' is, however, almost immediately followed by a round assertion that 'thou has not felt the lapse of hours!' (141), and the Scholar-Gipsy continues to be addressed as a being to whom the speaker has direct access. What is in question is not the realness of the subjective experience that the Scholar-Gipsy lives and may be met, but the reason for it, in which is felt to lie its value, and its compatibility with the world outside, being so completely different.

They key to the immunity of the Scholar-Gipsy from the assault of transience is felt to lie in two associated characteristics, namely his fugitive quality and his singleness of purpose. These are held to be connected in general, but particularly so with regard to the modern world which is disruptive in its multitudinousness to any self-dedication:

> *For what wears out the life of mortal men?*
> *Tis that from change to change their being rolls;*
> *Tis that repeated shocks, again, again,*
> *Exhaust the energy of strongest souls*
> *And numb the elastic powers.* (142–6)

The overcoming, or avoidance, of these influences would produce, if not actual immortality, at least a truth of spirit which is essentially timeless. The Scholar-Gipsy early and voluntarily left the world (though it does also rather seem that he could not make the grade), 'with powers Fresh, undiverted to the world without':

> *Thou hadst one aim, one business, one desire;*
> *Else wert thou numbered long since with the dead* (151–2),

and this having 'what we, alas! have not' is due not only to the individual quality of the Gipsy, but also to the fact that the preservation of the quality has since his day become immensely more difficult. It is notable that the speaker has now moved from 'I' to 'we'; he is summing up thoughts for a public and has closed with the poet. He contrasts the Scholar's life not individually with his own, but with what he perceives as typical, first of man, and then particularly of man at this time:

> *Free from the sick fatigue, the languid doubt,*
> *Which much to have tried, in much been baffled, brings.*
> *Oh life unlike to ours!*
> *Who fluctuate idly without term or scope.* (164–7)

The Scholar-Gipsy 'waitest for the spark from heaven' (reverting to the words of the earlier 'dream'); 'Ah! do not we, wanderer! await it too?' We, however, await it more with 'Sad patience, too near neighbour to despair', for 'None has hope like thine!' (195–6)

Behind this contrast lies Arnold's friend, the poet Arthur Hugh Clough. He is not represented by the Scholar or by the conception of contemporary life, but his relation to these contrasted values fascinated Arnold as he himself attempted to define his own predicament and to clarify his own purpose. Clough resigned his Oriel Fellowship in 1848 on the point of principle that he could not subscribe to the Thirty-Nine Articles, but no doubt also disturbed by the contrast of academic life with the turmoil of Chartism, Irish Famine, Revolution in France in the outside world. This was well before the poem was written (by which time he and Arnold were in London), but after the likely reference of the recollected scenes in *The Scholar-Gipsy*. But that is not to say that Arnold therefore saw him as an exemplar of 'singleness of mind', although he perhaps would have liked to do so, and in fact the exact reverse is the case. Recalling, perhaps, line 167 ('fluctuate idly') soon after finishing the poem he wrote to Clough,

> *You certainly do not seem to me suffiently to desire and earnestly strive towards knowledge-activity-happiness. You are too content to* fluctuate *– to be ever learning, never coming to the knowledge of the truth. This is why with you I find it necessary to stiffen myself and hold fast my rudder.*[4]

It was a nautical image to which Arnold was rather attached – and of some import to this poem. In 1849, defining his 'one natural craving' as a limited one ('not for profound thoughts, mighty spiritual workings etc. etc., but a distinct seeing of my way as far as my own nature is concerned'), he writes 'I can go thro: the imaginary process of mastering myself and see the whole affair as it would then stand, but at the critical point I am too apt to hoist the mainsail to the wind and let her drive.'[5] Here he is almost certainly thinking of religious meditation with withdrawal and ensuing knowledge of the Self culminating in religious trance, such as he found in the *Bhagavad Gita* (which he recommended to Clough in 1848 as distinguishing 'meditation and absorption – and knowledge'[6]). The Scholar-Gipsy, 'Rapt, twirling in thy hand a withered spray' and waiting 'for the spark from heaven to fall' (120), seems to be engaged in some such activity, having early left the world 'with powers Fresh, undiverted to the world without', and is therefore exempt from 'the sick fatigue, the languid doubt' of us who 'fluctuate':

> *But none has hope like thine!*
> *Thou through the fields and through the woods dost stray,*
> *Roaming the country-side, a truant boy,*
> *Nursing thy project in unclouded joy,*
> *And every doubt long blown by time away.* (196–200)

In Glanvill, the nature of the Scholar-Gipsy's 'project' which he pursues with such single purpose is to learn the 'secret' of the gipsies' mesmeric 'art', which, once gathered, he 'will to the world impart'. But in the poem either he has not found it or he has discovered that the quest is itself discovery, the 'way' is at once the 'destination'. The mesmeric art seems to be merely a starting point in history. The true purpose of the Scholar-Gipsy seems to be to seek religious and spiritual knowledge which will set the whole human predicament in perspective, and his very search seems to be an exemplary discovery for speaker and reader. In either case, he awaits the 'spark from heaven' (for 'it needs heaven-sent moments for this skill' – 50) and serves as an exemplar of a particular approach to life. In his chosen path he had a head-start, being born into a relatively Golden Age:

> *O born in days when wits were fresh and clear,*
> *And life ran gaily as the sparkling Thames;*
> *Before this strange disease of modern life,*
> *With its sick hurry, its divided aims,*
> *Its heads o'ertaxed, its palsied hearts, was rife.* (201–4)

He left Oxford for reasons quite different from those of Clough ('tired of knocking at preferment's door'). Being identified with the idealised countryside, he seems to be contrasted both with the Oxford of the 1840's (before Clough left) and with the modern world as Arnold sees it in the early 1850's (which neither he nor Clough has left). The preservation of his character depends on flight – 'Still fly, plunge deeper in the bowering wood' (207) – as Dido plunged back into the woods of Hades with Sychaeus her former lover, to avoid Aeneas whilst he declared he had had no choice but to follow his destiny and leave her. (The comparison is interesting; referring to Aeneas as the 'false friend', Arnold implies the placing of personal relationship above the supra-personal concerns on behalf of which Aeneas claimed to act. It is, after all, Aeneas, not Dido, who is dedicated, yet it is Dido who is compared to the Scholar-Gipsy in flight.) He is to 'fly our feverish contact' and 'the infection of our mental strife' – one recalls the 'contagion of the world's slow stain' (356) from which Adonais is 'secure' by death in Shelley's poem.

The Scholar-Gipsy is associated with values, however vague, which would presumably be found in neither the modern world nor the Oxford of the Seventeenth Century (however preferable) in a general and established way. He is exemplary at once of a personal ideal (with which might be contrasted the mass of humanity at any time, and of a virtue held to be more conceivable in an earlier age. This does not, of course, make for clarity of the 'pastoral' issues. Moreover, it is an assumption of the poem that, at least in his more personal role, he represents qualities not only missing from modern life but by their nature incompatible with it. Thus, exposed to the 'infection',

> *Soon, soon thy cheer would die,*
> *Thy hopes grow timorous, and unfixed thy powers,*
> *And thy clear aims be cross and shifting made;*
> *And then thy glad perennial youth would fade,*
> *Fade, and grow old at last, and die like ours.* (226–33)

It follows that the Scholar-Gipsy and what he represents cannot be introduced to or cultivated in such a world. Rather is it a question of leaving that world, by the adoption of some such meditational stance as the poet has already adopted in the first part of the poem but which was interrupted by the intrusion of the unpastoral reality ('But what – I dream!'). On many matters – our own personal values, our assessment of the justice of Arnold's description of his society and its relevance to our own, and on our sense as to whether or not he has sufficiently suggested the positive he would oppose to them – will depend our judgment on whether the 'pastoral', the essence represented in the Oxford countryside where the Scholar-Gipsy puts in his fleeting appearances, is merely escapist and false. For there is no doubt that the poem sets up opposed and incompatible worlds and invites a choice between them, whether it settles with sad stoicism in the world without inspiration, or whether, as I think, it tentatively suggests that, with a measure of 'flight' and detachment, there might in the modern individual, however far from the 'days when wits were fresh and clear', be still an infusion of what is lost.

Such is the position until the last two stanzas: the ideal spirit cannot be reconciled with 'this strange disease', the speaker near to despair urges even that which he most values, and of which he has been granted a glimpse, to fly away from the current corruption. It might be expected that, having abandoned the 'dream' and surveyed reality in its light, the speaker would then take the final step, open his eyes and see once more the nook in the half-mown field, nearer as it is to the ideal than have been his most recent broodings; we might, that is to say, have the opportunity to see the speaker as a dramatic protagonist and modify what he has said by the context of the whole. That would be the conventional ending. But Arnold does not adopt it. In fact, so far from moving outwards, he takes a further step inwards into one last spreading image of days more remote than any so far referred to, and in doing so he clinches the ambiguity of the Scholar-Gipsy as a characteristic of an age or a characteristic of the personality in any age.

The comparison in the last celebrated twenty-line sequence is primarily of the Scholar-Gipsy to a 'grave Tyrian trader' holding course 'indignantly' for Spain, the Iberian land of gipsies, where it successfully completes its mission ('undid his corded bales'), despite the threat of a new and distracting civilisation represented by the 'merry Grecian coaster freighted with grapes and Chian wine'. These 'young light-hearted masters of the waves' represent distraction, diversion from purpose, akin to the bathers above Godstow Bridge (91) from whom the Scholar-Gipsy flees just as much as he may be expected or advised to flee before the most solemn manifestations of a diseased modern world. The nautical image takes up those of 'fluctuation' already noticed in the letters to Clough.[7] The Trader snatches his rudder, controls his sail, as Arnold had suggested he felt obliged to do in meeting the personality of Clough or in the struggle for self-mastery. As the image is presented there is no presupposition of victory or loss; but of course our reading is conditioned by the knowledge that the Tyrian represents a culture which is doomed to be defeated by the merry and the new, and it is a presumption that the Scholar-Gipsy is more than hard-pressed in battling with the modern world – that, as we have noted, there is no possibility of compromise between them in the poem's terms.

The final simile thus suggests no solution and no return to the dramatic setting of the poem. It serves rather to sum up, to polarise, the opposed values of the reflection, but, and this is the important emphasis, it pictures not flight and escape stemming from weakness or a sense of futility (though 'indignantly' does not imply lasting success) but flight for a purpose which is in fact achieved despite the threat of 'the intruders'. It may be doubted whether the purpose of the Scholar-Gipsy is sufficiently clear or his link with an ideal countryside sufficiently essential for this image to work with entire conviction. But it is not too much, in view of the value which we have seen set on pastoral here and elsewhere, to see the threatened 'ancient home' of the Tyrian as the essence of the pastoral ideal, which is now opposed to reality, not only for the purpose of revealing the shortcomings of the real world, but because the modern and increasingly industrial world threatens to intrude. It is offered not merely as a criticism, but as some sort of alternative, whose practicality is felt to be rather doubtful. While there is indeed no sudden change in pastoral represented by the Romantics, 'pastoral' after the Mid-Nineteenth Century can never again be the same; it acquires a defensive aspect against such intrusion, and at its worst it comes to seem a sort of poetic Green Belt.

Thyrsis, unlike *The Scholar-Gipsy*, is a lament for a friendship. I say 'friendship' advisedly, for the deep relationship between Clough and Arnold is associated particularly with the 1840's (the period represented by the 'pastoral' of *The Scholar-Gipsy*), and both were conscious of a cooling of their affections in 1848 when in November Arnold visited Oxford and heard reactions to Clough's poem *The Bothie of Tober-na-Vuolich*. The paucity of references to the poem suggests that Arnold found it peripheral to what he considered the serious concerns of poetry and he was disgusted that the 'rest of that clique who know neither life nor themselves rave about your poem', which 'gave me a strong almost bitter feeling with respect to them, the age, the poem, even you'.[8] By early 1853, when Arnold had certainly been engaged on *The Scholar-Gipsy*, there were occurring accusations of neglect on Clough's side. Arnold declares that 'I cannot say more than that I really have clung to you in spirit more than to any other man' and that the 'estrangement' considered when the *Bothie* was published was 'merely a contemplated one and it never took place.' In a sense, he doth protest too much. We sense in the growing differentiation between his own outlook and that of Clough a gap which becomes increasingly hard to bridge. Arnold writes of Clough's letters (not extant) that 'I do not know that the tone of your letters exactly facilitates correspondence' and launches into a lengthy discussion of what each of them may have gained from their friendship. He 'looks back to that time (at Oxford) with pleasure' and declares Clough had always more to give the relationship than he had himself. The friendship was not over at the time of Clough's death, but meetings had inevitably become fewer and correspondence shorter. It had become more of an acquaintanceship sustained by memories and a sense of honour than a deeply live thing.

What runs through the letters to Clough, and indeed through any biography of Clough[9], is the contrast between the universal impression of Clough's enormous potential and the slightness of his actual achievement, or, as Arnold sees it, the dispersion of his powers (in total contrast to the singleness of purpose of the Scholar-Gipsy). To this, Arnold states, he has adjusted ('I had accustomed myself to think that no success of this kind, at all worthy of his great powers, would he now achieve'[10]) so that, with none of his other associates 'was the conviction of his truly great and profound qualities so entirely independent of any visible success in life which he might achieve'. Yet it is possible to doubt the wholeness of this adjustment. Indeed, Arnold himself admits that it hardly reached to the core of his being, since he goes on to say that 'now his early death seems to have reopened all the possibilities for him'.[11]

When Clough died, in November 1861 in Florence, he was 42 and Arnold 38. Their friendship was at its deepest when they were both at Oxford in their twenties. (In this respect there is some parallel of Tennyson and Hallam at Cambridge and Clough and Arnold at Oxford, and then their respective elegies.[12]) That, as Arnold perceptively implies, was as they were working out their mature identities, and at that time Clough could have a role which he could not afterwards sustain in relation to Arnold; 'this I am sure of; the period of my developement [sic] (God forgive me the d-d expression) coincides with that of my friendship with you so exactly that I am for ever linked with you by intellectual bonds – the strongest of all; more than you are with me; for your development was really over before you knew me', and what Clough's 'development' had arrived at was something quite inimical to Arnold, a 'poking and patching and cobbling ... looking for this and that experience...'[13]

The relevance of all this, if not the precise connection, to *The Scholar-Gipsy* seems clear. The Scholar-Gipsy represents the values idealised by the young Arnold, whilst Clough in a measure stands for the modern world. But for the purposes of *Thyrsis* the situation is rather different and Clough–Thyrsis has an understandably ambiguous role; it is as if he was once for the Scholar-Gipsy but subsequently deserted the cause. The elegy habitually contrasts the ideal and the actual, presenting the ideal in some sort of union with what is past. Moreover, it presents the tragedy of unfulfilment as imposed by early death rather than by some failure of the character and objects of the beloved. Yet Clough and Arnold had been in high degree identified in the 'Oxford dream' of the Forties and to that extent were one with, or in search of, the Scholar-Gipsy, that dream's representative. Hence *Thyrsis* as a pastoral monody called for a certain misrepresentation of the facts, and it is perhaps partly guilt at this misrepresentation which is responsible for the profound pathos; it is at once an elegy for how things once were and no longer are, and for how they might have been. But it is not a poem devoted solely, or even principally, to Clough, of whom it is confessedly partial – 'Still, Clough *had* this idyllic side, too; to deal with this suited my desire to deal again with that Cumner country: any way, only so could I treat the matter this time'.[14]

There is no 'setting' for *Thyrsis*, save what the monologue itself describes. The speaker is walking in Cumnor country, following the routes which he has followed before, on a warm winter evening – so much he tells us in the monody. But there is no attempt to make that monody especially plausible in the circumstances, as, for instance, with the 'roughness' of *Lycidas*, and indeed as a dramatic situation it is, with the complex Keatsian stanza and the patterned classical allusion, totally improbable so far as a sense of spontaneous effusion is concerned. The poem is indeed closer in some ways to the reflective pieces of Wordsworth or Coleridge, or to the *Odes* of Keats, than to the pastoral elegy since the immediate concern is not a real or imagined loss with urgent grief, but such a loss mediated through a larger theme. That theme is less of a search for consolation in immortality than of a search for assurance in changelessness[15]. If there can be found intact elements of the countryside as it was known with the friend – as, indeed, it was portrayed in *The Scholar-Gipsy* – then the spirit which they both contributed to that countryside, and associated with it, lives on, and the spirit of the friend with it. Essentially, it must be possible to recapture a previous (shared) experience from its setting. So the opening immediately relates the apparent transience of the country scenes to the transience of the person:

> *How changed is here each spot man makes or fills!*
> *In the two Hinkseys nothing keeps the same...*
> *See, 'tis no foot of unfamiliar men*
> *Tonight from Oxford up your pathway strays!*
> *Here came I often, often in old days –*
> *Thyrsis and I; we still had Thyrsis then.*

Introduced almost idly as the natural conclusion of such a walk is the 'signal-elm' which tops 'the hill behind whose ridge the sunset flames' and then, as the elm is yet unseen, the particular significance of the favourite tree is stated;

> *We prized it dearly; while it stood, we said,*
> *Our friend, the Gipsy-Scholar, was not dead;*
> *While the tree lived, he in these fields lived on.* (26–30)

The Scholar-Gipsy, then, whether in fact or only in fiction here, was an idea and a symbol shared by Thyrsis and the speaker, and the tree has been taken to be a guarantee of the Scholar-Gipsy's continued existence. For the sake of the poem, at least, it is particularly a communion of poetic purpose which is involved. Since the time when that communion existed (and well prior to his death), 'Thyrsis of his own will went away' (suggesting inaccurately that Clough ceased to write poetry after resigning his post at Oxford), whilst the speaker also went away under some unspecified compulsion, entering that same opposed world that he described in *The Scholar-Gipsy*. All this is described in terms of the abandonment of poetic pipes and it is significant that it is regretted fact of the past, whereas in the classical tradition the entry into the world of men is the great poetic purpose which will follow on pastoral diversion (as announced by Milton in *Epitaphium Damonis*, perhaps also in the 'pastures new' of *Lycidas* and, for example, in Virgil's *Eclogue IV*):

> *Here too our shepherd pipes we first assayed.*
> *Ah me! this many a year*
> *My pipe is lost, my shepherd's holiday!*
> *Needs must I lose them, needs with heavy heart*
> *Into the world and wave of men depart;*
> *But Thyrsis of his own will went away* (25–40)

In the poem, but hardly in fact, though Thyrsis 'loved each simple joy the country yields', his contentment was, in somewhat sentimental manner, overcast by a 'shadow':

> *He went; his piping took a troubled sound*
> *Of storms that rage outside our happy ground;*
> *He could not wait their passing, he is dead.* (48–50)

However this may be, there are really two matters for lament – not only is Thyrsis dead, but the speaker's relationship with him had already, in some degree died earlier. His actual death prompted a review of the relationship and its implications which is as much the subject of the poem as is the more conventional content of elegy.

The speaker then utters for fifty lines the conventional search for personal consolation, oblivious for the moment to the 'real' countryside around him. The cuckoo with his short stay (here shortened still further by having him depart in June) is taken to represent the transience of the seasons, and provides the excuse, in outlining the summer he misses, for the conventional 'flower passage':

> *Soon will the musk carnations break and swell,*
> *Soon shall we have gold-dusted snapdragon,*
> *Sweet-William with his homely cottage-smell* ... (63–6)

This identifies the 'summer' which could have been experienced by Thyrsis had he outlived the 'storms' (for there is a repeated, seemingly sentimental, connection between the 'storms' and Thyrsis's death) and represents also the floral tribute which he cannot experience. In the alternative to the 'Nature mourns' convention (in which the flowers unseasonably drop their buds and so forth), the spring is said to return, as Thyrsis cannot do – the passage (71–77) derives from the *Lament for Bion* (99–104) and, except that it is related to a lasting death rather than an insurmountable grief, can be compared with the 'spring' stanzas of *Adonais* (154–71). Its conventional nature seems to bring to the speaker's mind conventional pastoral elegy, represented by Virgil ('Time, not Corydon, hath conquered thee', (80) alludes to Virgil's *Eclogue VII* where Corydon defeats Thyrsis in a contest for song, though why Corydon should win has always been felt rather unclear); and by the *Lament for Bion* (115–26), whose Orphic lines suggest that the speaking poet (who declares himself unworthy) or the dead poet might sing to Proserpina, as did Orpheus, to secure release from Hades. It is, in origin, a large tribute to the powers of the dead poet, and so it serves also here. But that Sicilian pastoral world is rejected as a fiction unrelated to the modern world, and, no doubt, incidentally of no continued validity as a convention for the expression of grief of this nature:

> *O easy access to the hearer's grace*
> *When Dorian shepherds sang to Proserpine!* ...
> *She loved the Dorian pipe, the Dorian strain.*
> *But ah, of our poor Thames she never heard!*
> *Her foot the Cumnor cowslips never stirred;*
> *And we should tease her with our plaint in vain!* (91–100)

Traditional images of consolation are, then, of no avail, and the speaker returns to a consciousness of his surroundings in attempting to create a comparable memorial; for this, poetry itself, is also 'questing' (104). These surroundings, significantly and essentially, are shot with resemblances to the scenes of *The Scholar-Gipsy*. 'The Fyfield tree' (106) is that round which the girls danced before the Scholar-Gipsy presented them with 'store of flowers' (*The Scholar-Gipsy* 86), among which were 'purple orchises' (as here, line 115).[17] The bathers of *The Scholar-Gipsy* pass 'where black-winged swallows haunt the glittering Thames' (94), and here there are 'darting swallows' of 'the shy Thames shore' (126. The epithet 'shy' recalls the earlier poem.). Above Godstow Bridge were the mowers of hay (*The Scholar-Gipsy* 91) and here (129) the mowers 'Stood with suspended scythe to see us pass'. It is, plainly, an exercise in re-creation. The effort is to recall, when 'the ploughboy's team' has destroyed so much of the evidence (117), 'that forgotten time'; to find in the present walk that which Thyrsis and the speaker at least for a while held in common, representing the values of the Scholar-Gipsy, will both confer on Thyrsis a sort of immortality and restore the speaker to wholeness and purpose.

But these evidences' are all gone, and thou art gone as well!' (130). There now is felt that sense of isolation prelusive to vision in which, with the withdrawal of all activity and light, we first encounter the speaker of Gray's *Elegy*:

> *Yes, thou art gone! and round me too the night*
> *In ever-nearing circles weaves her shade* ... (131–2)

The night is itself emblematic, in this state of mind, of encroaching age and death:

> *I feel her finger light*
> *Laid pausefully upon life's headlong train;*
> *The foot less prompt to meet the morning dew,*[18]
> *The heart less pounding at emotion new,*
> *And hope, once crushed, less quick to spring again.* (136–40)

The 'quest' to identify what has not changed comes now into the context of the life-span, comes to represent a life-purpose, the search for 'The mountain tops where is the throne of Truth' (143),

> *And long the way appears, which seemed so short*
> *To the less practised eye of sanguine youth.* (141–2)

Death itself, as the end to the struggle and as the reunion, appeals:

> *And near and real the charm of thy repose;*
> *And night as welcome as a friend would fall.* (149–50)

This is the low-point, the dark night of the soul which precedes illumination, and that is at hand. The moment of vision in *Thyrsis* seems to be governed by the idea of the Scholar-Gipsy. As it was the Scholar's characteristic to 'flee' before activity and society, so it is a condition of the vision that the speaker enact in miniature that flight world. The Oxford hearties and hunters of the poem are not for this purpose any different from the 'millions of small (natures), newspapers, cities, light profligate friends' which lead to 'congestion of the brain'[19] in the modern world. In *The Scholar-Gipsy* the Scholar trailed his fingers in the water until the 'Oxford riders blithe' landed from the ferry, when immediately 'thou art seen no more' (*The Scholar-Gipsy*, 71ff). So now, when there is seen 'a troop of Oxford hunters going home As in old days, jovial and talking, ride!', the reaction of the speaker is that of the Scholar-Gipsy. It is as if he cannot be granted the vision until he has by his own action demonstrated precisely the survival of the Scholar-Gipsy which is the object of the quest:

> *Quick! let me fly, and cross*
> *Into yon farther field! – 'Tis done; and see,*
> *Backed by the sunset, which doth glorify*
> *The orange and pale violet evening-sky,*
> *Bare on its lonely ridge, the Tree! the Tree!* (156–60)

The Tree is described, significantly, as it has previously (12–13) been seen in the mind's eye – 'where the elm-tree crowns The hill behind whose ridge the sunset flames'. It recalls to us the 'favourite tree' of Gray's *Elegy* and the 'familiar elm' of Milton's *Epitaphium Damonis* – symbols of identity with nature whose origin is lost in the tree-worship of antiquity.[20]

The vision is but an 'omen', in that 'I cannot reach the signal-tree tonight' (and perhaps the 'quest' by definition can never be ended), but immediately it is referred to Thyrsis as evidence of the relationship's survival and its value held in common. He is asked to 'Hear it from thy broad lucent Arno-vale' (167). The idea is the sort of enthusiasm from which pastoral speakers are apt to awaken with a douche of reality, recalling bones being hurled in the sea and grief returning with the year. *Thyrsis* is no exception. As in *The Scholar-Gipsy* the dream of glimpses of the Scholar was interrupted at its climax by the perception that he must really be 'in some quiet churchyard lain' (137) – 'But what! – I dream' – so now (ironically, in view of the previous rejection of appeal to Proserpine which, however, he himself might have made) Thyrsis is in reality in a 'boon southern country' consorting with the mother of Proserpine, Demeter 'the great Mother'. He is enjoying a classical immortality remote indeed from Cumnor, hearing the 'immortal chants' of the silver-voiced Daphnis. The relationship, however, survives, as represented by the survival of the Scholar-Gipsy 'outliving thee', and evidenced by the existence of the Tree. To the values which it enshrines the speaker dedicates himself anew, recalling in *Lycidas* the dedication to the 'fame' that does not 'grow on mortal soil' (78):

> *A fugitive and gracious light he seeks,*
> *Shy to illumine; and I seek it too.*

> *This does not come with houses or with gold,*
> *With place, with honour and a flattering crew;*
> *Tis not in the world's market bought and sold.* (201–5)

It is not, we are to assume, mere escape, but withdrawal into contemplation or into action built upon self-knowledge (or into both), the lack of which self-realisation Arnold had criticised in Clough;

> *Not by refraining from action does man attain freedom from action. Not by mere renunciation does he attain supreme perfection ... Action is greater than inaction: perform therefore thy task in life. Even the life of the body could not be if there were no action ... Know therefore what is work, and also know what is wrong work. And know also of a work which is silence; mysterious is the path of work. The man who in his work finds silence, and who sees that silence is work, this man in truth sees the Light and in all his work finds peace.*[21]

The speaker then points to what has already been suggested, that the poem is a lament for and celebration of a friendship embodying certain values and a way of life, rather than an elegy for the death, primarily of an unfulfilled poet. The relationship in the form given to it in the poem was precarious, if not past, more than ten years before Clough died, and consequently of Clough as a whole, as he would be known to his contemporaries, there is not a great deal in the poem. As Arnold justly summed it up, 'One has the feeling, if one reads the poem as a memorial poem, that not enough is said about Clough in it.'[22] The reason is simply that whilst 'Thou too, O Thyrsis, on like quest was bound' (211) – the life's 'quest for what the Scholar-Gipsy represents being equivalent to the instanced 'quest' in the poem – it was only 'for a little hour' that 'thou wanderedst with me'. In that 'jocund youthful time' was Thyrsis's 'height of strength, thy golden prime!', and this 'virtue' still haunts the place with its spirit. But 'too soon' Thyrsis and his poetry 'learnt a stormy note of men contention-tossed, of men who groan', things incompatible (it seems) with poetry, and in consequence 'thou wast mute'. This world of contentious activity is evidently the same as the 'strange disease' which the Scholar-Gipsy was urged to flee in *The Scholar-Gipsy*.

One might have thought that there was here a straight opposition between Thyrsis and the speaker. But the difficulty experienced in gaining a sight of the Tree suggests that this is not so. The speaker seems during the poem to have pursued his life on lines which he prefers to the life of Thyrsis, to be torn, indeed, between lamenting his death or mourning his lapse. But in fact, of course, the speaker, if he retains a conviction of the value of the Scholar-Gipsy, feels out of touch with it. He also left this world, though he has claimed somewhat enigmatically that he was obliged to do so ('needs with heavy heart Into the world and wave of men depart' 138–9), whereas Thyrsis did so 'of his own will' (40). (It must be felt that the distinction is perfunctory, if not actually dishonest.) His 'home' is 'mid city-noise' ('Not, as with thee of yore, Thyrsis, in reach of sheep-bells', 223[23]) out of some unexplained necessity, and it does not appear that the same quest can be pursued there (though one wonders why it could not and what, then, is its worth). He complains of the 'rareness' of his 'visits' to the sacred spot as if his way of life were entirely outside his control rather than as if (as it must be) he has in practice for at least a while preferred other values. In fact, within the poem, the cases of Thyrsis and the speaker are not shown to be as dissimilar as the speaker tries to make out. If for different reasons, they are both remote from the Scholar-Gipsy now and have been so for quite some time. This befits the celebration of their friendship with common beliefs, even if it creates an awkward note when there is included mourning for Thyrsis's unhappy abandonment of these beliefs. In the light of this, what one would perhaps expect as an ending would be an unequivocal expression of the supreme worth of the Scholar-Gipsy as reflected in the countryside he is still conceived to haunt. Instead, we have lines somewhat ambiguous:

> Let in thy voice a whisper often come,
> To chase fatigue and fear:
> 'Why faintest thou? I wandered till I died.
> Roam on! The light we sought is shining still.
> Dost thou ask proof? Our tree yet crowns the hill,
> Our Scholar travels yet the loved hill-side.' (235–40)

The speaker last addressed Thyrsis ('not as with thee, of yore, Thyrsis!' – 232) and so it is the natural inference that he is still addressing Thyrsis and that it is into Thyrsis's voice that this 'whisper' will come. But Thyrsis, being dead, is beyond the need for fatigue and fear to be chased. Neither will he be in the town's 'harsh, heart-wearying roar'. In fact, then, at this climax, the speaker for the first time turns and addresses himself – thereby following another elegiac convention. He, certainly, lives 'mid city-noise', and he has been liable to 'faint' in the 'quest' during the poem. The voice is a reassurance, the expression of a sort of *alter ego*[23], and in it are curiously mingled the persons of the friendship – Thyrsis, the speaker, and the Scholar-Gipsy. It is the Scholar-Gipsy who 'wandered till I died' (that is, until after a lifetime of 'wandering' he was laid in the graveyard – *The Scholar-Gipsy*, 134–7), and in a sense it must also be he who whispers. It is the 'light' which both Thyrsis (for a while), the speaker and the Scholar-Gipsy (awaiting the 'spark from heaven') together 'sought'. The proof, which only the speaker can give, is offered that 'our' Tree is still there, and this is the Tree of Thyrsis and the speaker. 'Our Scholar' is still travelling the hillside, and therefore can perhaps not be whispering. Thyrsis himself can hardly 'prove' to the speaker the worth of an ideal he, Thyrsis, has been accused of rejecting. But, essentially, there is no single speaker; the components of the relationship merge again in prospect and the mergence has a benign influence on the humdrum world outside.

Thyrsis offers, then, mourning for the passing of a friendship and the values which it represented, but that mourning was prompted by the death of one of the friends, and to a degree the poem is also an elegy for him. The death brought also to mind the sense of unfulfilment, the contrast, that is, between Clough of *The Scholar-Gipsy* days and Clough later with his apparently sterile restlessness, to which Arnold claimed, somewhat ingenuously, to have adjusted. ('His early death seems to have reopened all the possibilities', that is, to have brought home the yawning gap between Clough's potential and Clough's achievement.[24]) Yet Arnold chose to make his poem a re-creation of what had been, its quality rather than its persons, an assertion that its spirit survived, rather than a more individual tribute or a lament for what death had cut off. He conceived that, whether it was 'his own will' or 'needs', it was not death that cut off the things he valued. Death, in fact, ironically brought about this one reacquaintance among visits increasingly 'rare'.

The poem itself is made strange (as of course it is also made superficially Victorian by its conception of 'nature' as apart) by the fact that the speaker is one who, for whatever reason, has given up what he celebrates. The celebration is therapeutic in a new way in that it does not so much provide, or pretend to provide, relief from pent-up grief; it provides rather demonstration that the source of poetic values is still alive, that he has still the 'power', can continue the 'quest' of poetry, and that what in appearance had been abandoned and died, in spirit may still live. But *Thyrsis* has things both ways – it mourns also the rareness of visits to the sources of the spirit, and it deplores the obliteration of the plough, yet it suggests no economic nor other connection between these things, so that it leaves somewhat obscure the extent to which it laments what might be regarded as inevitable and what is, perversely and with some self-pity, the consequence of personal choice. Then again, more deeply than Milton's exploitation of the conventional floral tribute, it delights in the paradoxical necessity of displaying what must be rejected; it declares the inaccessibility of Proserpine and her ignorance of the Thames, in a deeply memorable passage, and then it proceeds to assert that the 'omen' is inaudible because Thyrsis is beyond this earth listening to the 'immortal chants' of classical pastoral. Finally, it shows emphatically the orientation of elegy towards the mourner and, as we never come outside the speaker's mind (though we cannot help trying when he crosses that field and the want of a narrator is felt . . .), it leaves us in no doubt that the views and problems of the speaker are those of the poet addressing the reader. It is in this sense, not that of a speech accidentally overheard, that *Thyrsis* is a 'monody'.

VI

Tennyson – *In Memoriam*

The Poet and the Speaker

As expressive monument *In Memoriam* is perhaps supreme among these poems. It draws on conventions which it rejects. It dallies with possible consolations which it does not endorse. It is full of apology for the inadequacy of its tribute. It includes biographical details without a knowledge of which it is fairly unintelligible, yet in its handling of what (so far as Tennyson was concerned[1]) was an original stanza form, it is intricate, as it is in its revisions. It asserts and also denies that Nature's moods interact with those of the beholder. It declares throughout a modesty and an exclusive concern with the compulsive expression of grief which its scope and evident ambition deny. It is full of contradiction between one part and another which can yet be explained in terms of general drift. It employs all the themes and forces which we have noted, and yet (though there are perhaps relatively few parts of which it can be said 'this one could not be left out') it has the sense of a whole. In its composition and in its structure it is essentially accretive, and yet it leaves us unable to decide whether the accretion is due to accident, authorial honesty in respect of the 'facts', or a deliberate dramatic device. Probably, some of all three.

The poem, being 'elegies' (as Tennyson called them) assembled and written over more than sixteen years, purports to describe adjustment to grief within some two and a half years; that is, although the parts were not written in the order in which they appear, and more were written early than late, a process is presented in the poem which took, roughly, five times as long in real life as it is made to do in *In Memoriam*. (In brief, Hallam died in the autumn of 1833. The poems were written from then mainly until 1842, but also more desultorily until 1849. The structure of 'years' within the whole gives it a time-span of three Chistmases, but the biographical facts referred to go up to 1842. See also Chapter 5, note 12.)

In addition there is the *Epilogue* built on the marriage in 1842 of Tennyson's sister Cecilia to his friend Lushington, which occurred nine years after Hallam's death (as the poem accurately states) and seven and a half years before the end of the full period of composition. Moreover, events of certain date which are referred to in the poem do not correspond to the work's own rough sequence – thus the third Christmas in the poem, which should be 1835, must in fact be the fifth Christmas after Hallam's death since it takes place after the family have moved from Somersby in 1837. We have, in fact, instances of 'autobiography' incorporated which cannot, for the poem's purposes, be regarded as autobiography, and we have to decide how far this is a poem acceptable on its own terms, as a careful construction of a plausible change of mind, as fragments from the poetic diary of an imagined speaker concerning a fictional loss. To some extent, it is. But there may, I think, be circumstances – in particular the growth of literacy and the enormous increase in written and other records of individuals – which in modern times make the concept of an absolute distinction between 'autobiography' and 'art', 'poem and 'message' rather difficult to hold, or for the artist to observe without restricting himself to a very narrow field. Tennyson did not restrict himself to such a palace of art. Nor are his 'dramatic monologues' unambiguously examples of that form. *In Memoriam* goes far enough to suggest the self-contained piece working by example only on its readers, but it by no means goes the whole way.

The poem seems rather to exploit this ambiguity. When it is said that the flower passage in *Lycidas* (133–53), albeit a 'false surmise', is introduced 'to interpose a little ease', the speaker is commenting on the strain he is under and on the benefit of a respite, even one introduced on a false premise. But the poet also is speaking, commenting on the appropriateness to the whole of 'a little ease' inserted at this precise moment. The speaker comments, within the situation, on what he requires. The poem comments, from outside, on what his protagonist and also his reader might be thought to require. It is scarcely possible to separate speaker and poet; there is a sort of close ironic interplay between them, associated with the poetic beauty of what is nevertheless 'false'. The quest is as important as the destination. In *In Memoriam* the speaker and poet are still more tightly interwoven, for the speaker is more obviously and more consistently regarded as the creator of songs as well as the man with grief to face, and a good proportion of the poem is concerned with arguments, impressions, images which are little sooner uttered and (this is the important point) registered as part of the poem, than they are rejected and supplanted by others in the search. It is a case like that of the neo-Platonism in *Adonais*, where the steps are not taken away even when they have been climbed – and of course it is associated with the same dilemma, that the transcendent appears remote and the immanent appears subject to the transience from which the transcendent is exempt: 'only through time time is conquered'.

The speaker in the poem, if he is not the poet, is certainly a very articulate poet-figure. He speaks from a consciousness of the difference between a diary and a work of art. Tennyson's irony is that the one may be carefully regulated in its casualness to become the other.[2] The speaker insistently mentions the spontaneous and fugitive nature of his impressions. But he nonetheless gives them the form of rounded lyrics and, for all his apologies, they are there; pages in a diary are not missed out but remain part of the whole, with all its inconsistencies and afterthoughts. He claims to 'sing because I must' (xxi) and to be deficient in 'art', but, even as he is driven to 'express', he is also creating memorial; memorial, partly to the relationship of him and Hallam, whatever that may symbolise, but also shape and form to the grief which he claims wells from him uncontrollably, and to his progress with regard to it.

There is, as we have seen, a sense in which elegy veers towards paradox, in that with great deliberation it suggests a rough spontaneity, and by declaring the difficulties in the way of a memorial it constitutes one. The poetic device, which might be regarded as an exercise for 'distancing' grief in objective form, is elaborated not towards a hard purity but towards a suggestion of inevitable imperfection, and the effort of such elaboration is no less a discipline, and no more indicative of an absence of true feeling, than would be the other. Thus the declared 'artless tale' is not artless, though it may be a constructed impression of artlessness. The paradoxes stem from the presentation of a surrogate (traditionally a simple swain) for the poet, who attempts to do within the poem what the poet is doing by writing it. They are especially evident in *In Memoriam*, where the surrogate is not so much unsophisticated as distraught, even unbalanced. A collection of 'elegies' was assembled into a representation of the 'Way of the Soul' (as Tennyson referred to it). 'I did not write them with any view of weaving them into a whole, or for publication, until I found that I had written so many', and again to James Knowles he commented, 'The general way of its being written was so queer that if there were a blank space I would put in a poem'.[3] The thing arose in a casual manner. But it was also designed to give the casual manner of one who has more on his mind than he can cope with. To what extent the character of a 'diary' arises from the work's origin, and to what extent from Tennyson's exploitation of its origin for dramatic purposes, we can hardly tell. But, when he did 'weave them into a whole', the wayward and incidental nature of their composition over so long a period could be seen to image the vacillations of someone faced with overwhelming loss; in some degree, the obscurity of the structure, its habit of moving in leaps and gaps, plausibly mirrors the movements of such a person's mind.

There are a number of reasons for the self-consciousness of the poet-figure, which takes for the most part the form of deprecation and apology. As we first meet it, in the *Prologue* (in fact a late addition, untitled by Tennyson, and summing up rather than introducing the poem), it is directed at a rejection of poetic expressions of a grief which has been outgrown:

> *Forgive these wild and wandering cries,*
> *Confusions of a wasted youth...*

The appeal is nominally to the 'Strong Son of God, immortal Love'. But it is also to the reader, to prepare him (as, in fact, the final stage in Tennyson's weaving into a dramatic whole, his 'distancing' of his former self) for what may seem excessive feeling; since the nature of Hallam and the poet's relations with him are beyond definition, the normal criteria of appropriate emotions may seem to be exceeded. And, as he begins, so he ends. The *Epilogue* (again, untitled by Tennyson, and added late, though before the *Prologue*) sets the whole friendship into a larger perspective and, within the poem's time-scheme, looks back on expressions of grief of six or more years earlier;

> *For I myself with these have grown*
> *To something greater than before;*
>
> *Which makes appear the songs I made*
> *As echoes out of weaker times,*
> *As half but idle brawling rhymes,*
> *The sport of random sun and shade.*

'The sport of random sun and shade' refers to definitions of the speaker and his expressions within the poem. The truth cannot, it seems, be stated plainly. Words mislead. Particularly is this felt towards the start of the poem where grief is a choking darkness through which there are as yet no chinks – before even the body of Hallam has been brought back to England for burial. Then

> *I sometimes hold it half a sin*
> *To put in words the grief I feel;*
> *For words, like Nature, half reveal*
> *And half conceal the Soul within* (v).

Poetry, with its regularity, is a 'narcotic', a 'sad mechanic exercise'. To it, as to self-absorption in grief, the speaker is addicted although he knows the process is a confusion:

> *In words like weeds, I'll wrap me o'er,*
> *Like coarsest clothes against the cold:*
> *But that large grief which these enfold*
> *Is given in outline and no more* (v).

Not only, in the early stages, are the songs a drug, they are also ineffective (save from the point of view of expression). As a memorial they are nothing, for 'thy deepest lays are dumb Before the mouldering of a yew' (lxxvi). Moreover, they are mistrusted; contemplating a vision of Hallam's immortality, he ends wryly,

> *So hold I commerce with the dead;*
> *Or so methinks the dead would say;*
> *Or so shall grief with symbols play*
> *And pining life be fancy-fed.* (lxxxv)

It is a frequent theme that the use of words for expression begets self-delusion – words contain, suggest, always more than the bare meaning.

This mistrust of words, the sense that they can blind, mislead, and drug, leads to repeated statements that poetry's power is either consolatory, through spontaneous self-expression (which, later, is qualified and itself mistrusted), or revelatory by a flash of suggestion; it cannot, though so much of the poem is in fact argumentative, argue or prove. Self-expression deliberately pursued in this way is presumably an indulgence of the order of the narcotic, and indeed there is criticism of it from that point of view. But it is also conceived as something more outward-looking, essentially a release – a release which, as demonstrated by the persistent introspective debate of the whole, cannot be sustained, but this is for a while a benefit in the absence of actual consolation. Thus, taking the grasses from the grave and in a very pastoral manner making pipes of them, the speaker will not accept that he makes 'parade' of self-pity or 'would make weakness weak'. He sings rather under compulsion, to which any question of self-justification is beside the point;

> *I do but sing because I must,*
> *And pipe but as the linnets sing.* (xxi)

In the inability of words to express, as also in the necessity to make utterance in ignorance, he is as 'An infant crying for the light And with no language but a cry' (liv). Alternatively, he is not worthy of Parnassus or Urania, but only of 'my Melpomene', the muse of his small personal tragedy,

> *And owning but a little art*
> *To lull with song an aching heart.* (xxxvii)

The 'poor flower of poesy' which, in conventional fantasy, he proposes to plant on a tomb which does not yet even exist (viii), can constitute no adequate poetic memorial, but follows rather an expressive purpose:

> *I leave thy praises unexpressed*
> *In verse that brings myself relief,*
> *And by the measure of my grief*
> *I leave thy greatness to be guessed* (lxxv)

Yet even expression is a qualified benefit only. The most he can gain from it is 'a doubtful gleam of solace' as contrasted with a joyless spring (xxxviii); 'other griefs within', 'tears that at their fountain freeze', are unaffected, though 'lighter moods' may 'out of words a comfort win' (xx). Of the status of poetry itself he is uncertain. He believes that 'in these fading days', even if he could render tribute in words, it would not last but be merely a 'little dust of praise' (lxxv). 'Mortal lullabies of pain' may serve to 'bind a book' or 'line a box'. In the circumstances, though he sounds unconvinced, the speaker will somehow transcend the memorial function by the expressive:

> *But what of that? My darkened ways*
> *Shall ring with music all the same;*
> *To breathe my loss is more than fame,*
> *To utter love more sweet than praise.* (lxxvii)

Thus we are faced with a poet-figure who has on the whole a most limited belief in poetry. As in the case of *Lycidas*, the purpose of poetry is somehow involved in the personal loss (though Tennyson does not present Hallam as a poet here, despite several borrowings from his work), and the making of the elegy is peculiarly onerous in that the poet is called on for an outstanding work of tribute at exactly the time when he is quite unable to compose so positive a thing. Much of *In Memoriam* is concerned with the growth away from the purely expressive view of poetry with which the speaker starts out. He is not able to substitute till the very end a poetry of statement and affirmation (and even then leaves us a little uneasy), partly because he does not trust words as exact units of meaning to convey such notions, 'for words, like Nature, half conceal and half reveal'. Hence he is left with the possibilities of suggestion, implication and indirectness and, because it seems that words fix in a falsity, whereas truth is glimpsed in a flash, because at best words are images and 'matter-moulded forms of speech' (xcv), he is committed to seemingly spontaneous and intuitive insights – which indeed consort perfectly with the 'accidental' structure, the 'weaving' of the parts into some sort of continuity. The 'brief lays, of Sorrow born' are not such as 'close grave doubts' or 'propose answers', but rather

> *Short swallow-flights of song, that dip*
> *Their wings in tears, and skim away.* (xlviii)

They produce 'random influences'

> *Like light in many a shivered lance*
> *That breaks about the dappled pools.* (xlix)

They are, and produce, a 'seeming-wanton ripple' and the playing of a 'tender-pencilled shadow' (xlix).

Here, then, we have an irony essential to *In Memoriam*. From the short, spontaneous outflowings which serve primarily a relieving purpose, but which may convey fleeting perceptions of the truth, is constructed a positive memorial which appears to have been contrived by Tennyson from a viewpoint rather different from that which his speaker adopts for much of the time. Whilst there is not complete consistency, this is one of the major themes. As we have noted, two rejections, or at least qualifications, of the songs of grief occur in the *Prologue* and *Epilogue*, which we know to have been written after Tennyson had decided to 'weave' the 'elegies' together, and these rejections are anticipated by the affirmations of the last twelve or so parts. In the *Epilogue* he claims to have outgrown the earlier rhymes which are (recalling xlix) 'the sport of random sun and shade', and in the *Prologue* we have a prayer to forgive them as 'Confusions of a wasted youth'. The two rejections illustrate how far he has come along the 'way of the soul' – the *Epilogue* in fact suggests that the progress and 'growth' is partly the result of mere 'summers that are flown' (an unavoidable course of nature in which indifference would be hard to distinguish from genuine acceptance, and in which the idea of the 'way of the soul' seems somewhat compromised) rather than of development within the two and a half years. But it seems clear that both *Prologue* and *Epilogue* are meant to show more fully accomplished a growth which was already begun within the body of the poem.

The Dying of Regret

The prayer in the *Prologue* ('Forgive my grief for one removed') indicates one of the key-words in the progress of speaker and poem. At the time, 'grief' was a word still used very generally of suffering, pain and distress, rather than more exclusively of the sorrow aroused by bereavement, and as such it applied to things which could be alleviated or whose cause could be removed. Whilst we can see by a rather tortuous reasoning through grief to idolisation, whether of the self or of the bereaved, that grief might appear something culpable, we do not, being conditioned to the generalisation of states of mind and affects high and low, readily see it as a sin. But it is rather in this light, coupled with an exaltation of the self and of Hallam, that Tennyson views grief by the end of the poem, an indulgence more serious than it might seem to the modern reader.

The speaker has with grief a sort of love-affair, for which he used physical imagery. He requires 'sorrow' to be 'no casual mistress, but a wife' (lix), a replacement for what his heart, frequently said to be 'widowed', has lost. Grief is for him the representation of the being with which he was identified and which has gone.[4] Keeping grief, which enshrines memory, alive, seems to amount to keeping 'so sweet a thing alive' (xxxv). Love and grief are not inseparable, but it is felt that they must be made to be ('Let Love clasp Grief lest both be drowned' – i). The more shattering is felt to be the grief (for there *is* an element of parade here, demonstrating something to the world to gain conviction), the greater will love appear – 'And by the measure of my grief/I leave thy greatness to be guessed' (lxxv). He is told he 'loves to make parade of pain' and can only reply, as we have seen, that he 'sings because he must' (xxi).

To this perpetuation of Hallam by means of grief is opposed the recognition, in typically doubtful fashion and for the while contradicted, 'O last regret, regret can die!', or, as *Adonais* had put it:

> *Alas! that all we loved of him should be,*
> *But for our grief, as if it had not been,*
> *And grief itself be mortal! (181–3)*

Regret does not die. In a direct echo, by the *Epilogue* we are told 'Regret is dead, but love the more.' Regret 'dies' perhaps primarily because a larger and less personal conception of love emerges, because, that is, of a devlopment of faith ('which came first?' is the sort of chicken-and-egg question which the poem's structure and composition realistically pass by). The *Epilogue* refers to the passing of time as a factor in this, and such is also an impression given by the poem itself – both the passing of time and the finding of trust are there, as dramatic realism demands and as, perhaps, autobiographical accuracy ensured that they would be. But we have, I think, less the impression that the dying of grief is a question of erasure by time, a failure of memory, than the feeling that it is one of a number of manifestations of change which appear gradually together; the love of Hallam, instead of being a single exclusive obsession (and instead, equally, of being superseded – for that is the fear), takes its place as one element of a more outward-looking, less defensive mind.

The reorientation is expressed in a series of declarations which seem at first, like the clinging to grief, to be a sort of bravado not corresponding to the facts, but are gradually restated, less clamantly, as part of a coherent outlook. For example, first (but already when the depths have partly been left) there is the dream that 'there would be Spring no more', here (lxix) virtually a conceit rather than a despairing statement of the 'Nature's unnaturalness' theme of a spring which is autumn or which will not come out of winter. In the 'noisy town' he puts on his head a crown of thorns and is mocked by one and all. This seems to mark a dawning perception of the disproportion of his obsession (earlier, in xxi, he is oblivious to criticism); when he is consoled by 'an angel of the night' (whom the imagery suggests to be Hallam, though Tennyson stated that 'the Divine Thing in the gloom brought comfort'), 'the voice was not the voice of grief' – though this was at this stage 'hard to understand'. Later, considering the proposed marriage of Hallam with his sister Emily, the bearing of children, and his own putative role then as 'honoured guest', he moves from that domestic situation to contemplate the end when Christ

> Would reach us out the shining hand
> And take us as a single soul (lxxxiv);

but he rejects this recurrent image of future involvement and union (which is typical of the speaker in the state of 'grief') as a fantasy of a regret all but outgrown:

> What reed was that on which I leant?
> Ah! backward fancy, wherefore wake
> The old bitterness again, and break
> The low beginnings of content,

and he prefers that grief should be left sleeping, associated as it is with 'bitterness'.

Pursuing this outward movement still further in the poem to Edmund Lushington which mentions his own future bride, he feels open conflict between the determined 'I count it crime To mourn for any overmuch', and the reminder by the seasons of 'My old affection for the tomb'. The latter urges that he seek 'a friendship for the years to come'. Typically, this is not a straight advice that grief is past and he may as well now look for friends in a positive way; it is a (to him) treacherous assertion of the total death of Hallam – he should look for friends elsewhere, since Hallam is utterly dead. Grief's straight answer to this is that if you form a new love you must have forgotten or even belittled the old one ('let love clasp grief lest both be drowned'). But, at this stage in the poem, the speaker does not give such an answer. In fact he calmly assesses his present state;

> I could not, if I would, transfer
> The whole I felt for him to you ...
>
> My heart, though widowed, may not rest
> Quite in the love of what is gone,
> But seeks to beat in time with one
> That warms another living breast. (lxxxv)

The 'old affection of the tomb' suggests he seek new friends because all is over (the right deed for the wrong reason). In fact, the old affection is not wilting and is still a 'prime passion'; but the very crossing of the mind of the idea of new relationships indicates that the hold of grief is less, and there is a wish for company to consort with it.

There is a similar closeness of argument in the poem on the Third Christmas (cv), the first away from Somersby with all its associations of youth with Hallam, and in that about the New Year which follows it. The predominant quality of the Christmas is its 'strangeness'. This arises superficially from the change of address, but that is made to symbolise change in general and in particular the possibility of change in grief;

> No more shall wayward grief abuse
> The genial hour with mask and mime;
> For change of place, like change of time,
> Has broke the bond of dying use (cv).

And, as there is to be no disparity between the mind and the outside world, no maintaining of an 'ancient form' and custom when its 'spirit breathes no more', the summer is felt to be 'sleeping', and its long sleep is accepted without complaint;

> Long sleeps the summer in the seed;
> Run out your measured arcs, and lead
> The closing cycle rich in good.

The ensuing New Year poem (cvi) is a notably rhetorical exploration of the theme of 'ring out' what is past and should be past, and 'ring in' what is to come and should be good. There is a note, certainly, of shallow Victorian optimistic hymning here. Yet it is also dramatically appropriate as bravura, for this is not a poem in isolation, but the expression of a mood in the context of the whole, in which

> Ring out the grief that saps the mind,
> For those that here we see no more (cvi)

means not that all grief is gone or should be gone, but that the notion of there being no grief can now be entertained. There is a similar simplicity, a bravura, in the declaration that

> I will not eat my heart alone,
> Nor feed with sighs a passing wind (cviii).

These are flirtations, performances, statements in advance of their coming true. But in time they do come true, and then we look back, comparing Christmas with Christmas, anniversary with anniversary, and note the seeds some time before. Thus by the third spring, the speaker is for the first time (cxv) able to respond to harmony in Nature, for 'in my breast Spring wakens too', and spring cries 'through the sense to hearten trust In that which made the world so fair' (cxvi). Although 'regret' also wakens (as it does in *Adonais* (155); 'Grief returns with the revolving year'), it is not, he recognises fully, 'all regret' that stirs:

> *Yet less of sorrow lives in me*
> *For days of happy commune dead;*
> *Less yearning for the friendship fled*
> *Than some strong bond which is to be.*

There then follow the sections in which the conception of an emergent race of more perfect man, of which Hallam may be seen as herald, triumphs over the apparent purposelessness of geological change. Out of them emerges a sort of salvage operation in which a personal faith (based on, or strongly confirmed by, an idea of union which we have yet to consider), a subjective certainty, appears to represent the assurance in the light of which past fears can be seen (within and for this poem – not necessarily as a 'message', but as an example to be considered in context). At times, perhaps, there seems a little naiveté about this, for example in

> *Whatever I have said or sung,*
> *Some bitter notes my harp would give,*
> *Yea, though there often seemed to live*
> *A contradiction on the tongue,*
>
> *Yet hope had never lost her youth* (cxxv).

If he is serious, the calculating artist, overseeing the whole, appears to be overplaying his hand; it does not improve the poem, dramatically considered or otherwise, for us to try to believe that there existed only a 'contradiction on the tongue', and it is straining credibility to suggest that the speaker at this late stage is deceiving himself because he is unsure of his newly found unity. However this may be, *In Memoriam* does move with gathering assurance to its conclusion – and then to its *Epilogue* which asserts that grief was outgrown but love became more, that this memory is not incompatible with new relationship. I do not think that, if the poem is viewed dramatically, such assertions are inappropriate.

Development appears also in the treatment of the conventional relation of Nature to events and, essentially in this poem, to the poet-figure's mind for, though he makes some use of the old notion that nature herself is unseated by so momentous a death as the one being celebrated, and the seasons grow awry, it is as an appearance, as a possible delusion of one overwhelmed. Tennyson is far more intent on the dissociation of Nature and the speaker's mind, by which apparently external observation is locked in subjectivity and governed by mood, than is any of the poets we have considered hitherto. Nature is for the most part indifferent herself, and without mood, save by figures of speech which can be put down to the disturbed mind. Her apparent moods are as often contributed by the observer, contrasted as they may be with the sap rising. What is sought, and sought partly with a feeling that the 'pastoral' association is too good to be true, is an abandonment of this disjunction, this tension between the object and the subject, not so much a union as a clarification of perception. So Nature is either a wholesome cycle from which the speaker feels excluded, or it is one manifestation of the huge impersonal force which lies behind aeons of geological change and the coming and going of species of which man is but one.

At the beginning of the poem, the conventions of Nature mourning and of the mind unhinged from the Natural order are far more prominent than they later become, and the contrast between mood and fact, where there is one, is expressed starkly and without hesitation. We can see the difference even in the two 'yew-tree' poems, both of which occur early on. In the first (ii) the yew, as embodiment of grasping death and changelessness, corresponds with the state of grief and is contrasted with Nature as a whole. Gazing on the tree, the speaker seems to fade, his vital forces to run down, so that he mysteriously enters the spirit and identity of the tree and 'grows incorporate' with it. Its distinctive feature is that it is, as is the mind, unable to participate in the variety of Nature:

> *The seasons bring the flower again,*
> *And bring the firstling of the flock;*
> *And in the dusk of thee, the clock*
> *Beats out the little lives of men.*
>
> *O not for thee the glow, the bloom,*
> *Who changest not in any gale,*
> *Nor branding summer suns avail*
> *To touch thy thousand years of gloom.*

As Love is invited to clasp Grief, so the speaker struggles to clasp, to become inseparable from, the yew. The poem suggests dramatically in its place in the poem the blankness of mourning immediately after bereavement, though it was not in fact written early. The second yew-tree poem (xxxix) was written late indeed (1st April 1868), and it seems to have been added and so placed in order to offer one of the first suggestions of a shifting of despair. Typically, it suggests a sort of spring of the mind, only to declare that there can be no such thing, but, typically also, the entry of the idea into the poem in this negative form prepares for its entry later as a full positive. The subject is introduced indirectly – the yew responds to a blow from a cane with 'fruitful cloud of living smoke' – and then developed by way of the tree's flower:

> To thee too comes the golden hour
> When flower is feeling after flower (xxxix).

One notes the tentativeness as well as the sense of forward movement in 'feeling'. But then 'sorrow' 'whispers' the usual answer of elegy in its 'grief' phase – that summer is followed by winter, and the cycle of the seasons cannot provide support for positive conclusions:

> Thy gloom is kindled at the tips,
> And passes into gloom again. (xxxix)

In a rather similar image, when Shelley's 'Grief made the young Spring wild' she 'threw down her kindling buds, as if she Autumn were' (*Adonais* 137).

The violent unseasonableness suggested by Shelley finds a parallel in the theme of Nature's upheaval which the speaker pours forth on the first anniversary of Hallam's death, itself in autumn:

> Day when my crowned estate begun
> To pine in that reverse of doom
> Which sickened every living bloom,
> And blurred the splendour of the sun. (lxxii)

The coincidence of storm and anniversary, autumn in one aspect with autumn in the aspect of destruction, indicates both a state of mind and the mind's resort to a figure of rhetoric in the frustrated attempt to find something to blame for its misery. The character of Nature rests with the observer and with chance – Nature is itself indifferent. Thus, with its 'quick tears that make the rose pull sideways', the day's catastrophe is contrasted with other possible aspects of an autumn dawn, which do not correspond with the speaker's mood but suggest even now that all hope is not dead:

> Who mightst have heaved a windless flame
> Up the deep East, or, whispering, played
> A chequer-work of beam and shade
> Along the hills, yet looked the same. (lxxii)

Related, but characterised by a frozen and patterned calmness, are the assertions of waking spring with a winter of grief which will not pass. The first spring – that which is noted in the yew – is remarked in passing reference but without a set-piece of contrast; it is as if the state of grief is so deep that spring light scarcely penetrates it, the personality derealised and only half-conscious of the outside world:

> *The purple from the distance dies,*
> *My prospect and horizon gone.*
>
> *No joy the blowing season gives,*
> *The herald melodies of spring,*
> *But in the songs I love to sing*
> *A doubtful gleam of solace lives* (xxxviii)

The second spring is contrasted even in tense; the present of the first winter and spring, beyond which the speaker cannot hope to see, is replaced by the past. Amid hints of new relationships and hopes, there is the feeling that the New Year hangs back as a future to be born. Thus, as we have seen, in lxxxv 'my old affection of the tomb' tries to dispel the notion of 'a friendship for the years to come', but the very appearance of that notion is an indication of the weakening of the grasp of the yew. In lxxxiii a short and beautiful flower-passage is expressive of a feeling that grief is out of tune with the seasons – now more clearly external to the observer – and will, with time, reenter harmony:

> *Can trouble live with April days,*
> *Or sadness in the summer moons?*
>
> *Bring orchis, bring the foxglove spire,*
> *The little speedwell's darling blue,*
> *Deep tulips dashed with fiery dew,*
> *Laburnum, dropping-wells of fire.*
>
> *O thou, new-year, delaying long,*
> *Delayest the sorrow in my blood;*
> *That longs to burst a frozen bud*
> *And flood a fresher throat with song* (lxxxiii).

It cannot, yet; but the prayer that it might do is very different from the blank assertions of the yew in ii, or of 'dark house' in vii. Again, in lxxxvi, the same spring is asked to

> *fan my brows and blow*
> *The full new life that feeds thy breath*
> *Throughout my frame . . .*

Finally, in the third spring (in fact of 1838 rather than of 1836), there is still present the dissociation, but the ambiguity is further heightened. The spring itself is celebrated in more of a paeon,

> *Now fades the last long streak of snow,*
> *Now burgeons every maze of quick*
> *About the maze of flowering squares, and thick*
> *By ashen roots the violets grow.*

The birds that 'build and brood' bring to mind Hopkins's line, 'birds build – but not I build'[5], but now as a contrast. There is the hesitancy still at accepting April, but there is a full response to its new life:

> and in my breast
> Spring wakens too; and my regret
> Becomes an April violet,
> And blossoms like the rest. (cxv)

The conceit is a little pat, as a tribute to a grief which has lost its full frost, tagged on for the sake of a still willed consistency of regret in the face of a deep realisation of life stirring in all things. So it is also in the following poem, which almost resolves the conflict:

> Is it, then, regret for buried time
> That keenlier in April wakes,
> And meets the year, and gives and takes
> The colours of the present prime?
>
> Not all: the songs, the stirring air,
> The life re-orient out of dust,
> Cry through the sense to hearten trust
> In that which made the world so fair . . .
>
> Yet less of sorrow lives in me
> For days of happy commune dead;
> Less yearning for the friendship fled,
> Than some strong bond which is to be (cxvi)

Nature is, then, perhaps not wholly indifferent, but what healing power she exerts is inseparable from the passing of time. It was but a 'dream' that 'nature's ancient power was lost', and not merely a fancy that 'the voice was not the voice of grief' (lxix). It is, as it were, a symptom of grief that makes the mind to be, and to want to be, indistinct from Nature; yet it is not until the mind is partly healed that its true involvement with Nature, its unbiased kinship with the seasons, can appear. It was the unnatural state of the observer rather than any errancy on the part of Nature which was responsible for the alienation between them, and the 'healing' seems to depend on acts of will and minute changes of attitude in several directions which can neither be attributed to nor wholly divorced from 'nature's power'.

Tennyson appears not to be under the pressures working on, for example, Arnold and Hardy, to re-create the lost past, and therefore he does not consistently relate such a vision to an idealised 'nature'. Compared with these poets, his speaker has a fundamentally different stance in which, at the start, consciousness of present grief dominates all else and, later, external stimuli prompt the recall of that grief, and the charting of its course, rather than its origin. He rarely recalls the past in attempted transcendence of loss. He believes rather that some sort of communication and contact can be restored through relating himself to the various possibilities of Hallam's present state, and he never abandons that approach despite the fact that the climax of the poem includes an element of 'recollection'.

Yet there is re-creation of a sort in *In Memoriam*. It takes the form of revisitation (as it does with Arnold and Hardy) but not, so far as we know, of deliberate pilgrimage. The speaker does not seem impelled to seek out past association. When he is confronted by a familiar scene it is not possible for him to make of the past a lasting subjective present. As he looked round Trinity College, Cambridge, visiting what had been Hallam's room, it was as much the discontinuity as the continuity which struck him; it all 'felt the same but not the same' (lxxxvii). The visits to familiar haunts rather reinforce than dispel the sense of a gulf, and there is guilt in the feeling that he intrudes on a scene to which he has lost all claim to belong. This is apparent in the first 'dark house' poem where the Hallam family home, which once was visited 'waiting for a hand' (a symbol repeatedly used of meeting, and possible reunion with, Hallam), is revisited after a sleepless night,

> *And like a guilty thing I creep*
> *At earliest morning to the door.* (vii)

What above all is apparent is emptiness, de-realisation, in which ordinary life is a remote happening which can make no sense:

> *He is not here; but far away*
> *The noise of life begins again,*
> *And ghastly through the drizzling rain*
> *On the bald street breaks the blank day.* (vii)

At a second revisitation, inserted into the poem at a late stage (rather as was the second yew-tree poem), the depressing urbanisation is not felt and, as the imagination is now freed, 'in my thoughts ... I take the pressure of thy hand':

> *Doors where my heart was used to beat*
> *So quickly, not as one that weeps*
> *I come once more; the city sleeps;*
> *I smell the meadow in the street.*
>
> *I hear a chirp of birds; I see*
> *Betwixt the black fronts long withdrawn*
> *A light-blue lane of early dawn,*
> *And think of early days and thee* (cxix)

Though plainly there is a difference of mood, still it cannot be said that the association of the place produces any distinct sensation that Hallam is alive.

Yet we may wonder what accounts for such a change of mood, and the freedom of sensibility which can now 'smell the meadow in the street'. In fact, a number of factors, some of which we have already noted, interact, but the prime ones are a visionary experience, to be considered shortly, and the experience of moving from Somersby to High Beech, Epping, in the summer of 1837 (which in the poem occurs immediately after the 'second anniversary' of the death (in xcix) and so, in the internal time-scheme, occurs rather in early summer, 1836). The sections on the move are critical in that, coinciding with other independent elements working towards re-orientation, they show the change of address as enforcedly an end to what appear the persistently wounding effects of association with surroundings with which Hallam had been one. For though surroundings would produce no sense of survival in the present, they did contribute powerfully to the survival of the past, to the 'grief' from which the speaker is slowly emerging.

To begin with, the scenes are inseparable from the lost friend, though they convey no sense of his immediate presence. They are described in terms of a simple stability, recalling Eighteenth Century pastoral in its generality and its diction:

> No gray old grange, or lonely fold,
> Or low morass and whispering reed,
> Or simple style from mead to mead,
> Or sheepwalk up the windy wold . . .
>
> Nor runlet tinkling from the rock;
> Nor pastoral rivulet that swerves
> To left and right through meadow curves,
> That feed the mothers of the flock . . . (c)

These are the situations, described by negatives because they are example of 'no place that does not breathe' memories of Hallam (and which will be no more), abandoned by the move:

> And, leaving these, to pass away,
> I think once more he seems to die.

Again, there is the notion that the whole homeship will die, 'unwatched', 'unloved', 'uncared for' (the functions of grief),

> Till from the garden and the wild
> A fresh association blow,
> And year by year the landscape grow
> Familiar to the stranger's child. (ci)

The conception of an inheritor is analogous to the tentative admission of the possibility of finding new friends. It is the start of the way out, for whilst 'our memory fades From all the circle of the hills', whilst indeed the move represents transience, the garden will be taken over by another, with 'fresh association', and in the same it can be envisaged that the new home is also to be occupied by what might seem 'a stranger race'.

As they move, the speaker engages in a final skirmish;

> *Two spirits of a diverse love*
> *Contend for living masterdom*

of the mind (cii). The 'spirits' are identified as Tennyson's father and Hallam. Alternatively, they are 'the love of the native place' and 'the memory of AHH'.[6] But either way, there is an irony in that the contention between them is not quite what the reader expects; this is not a struggle between the home and the future, but between forces of kinship and of friendship, as to which has the stronger hold through the house at Somersby. It is, in fact, an image of 'regret' (that word virtually identical to 'grief' in representing an exclusive and inward-looking memory); but it is also a somewhat strained conceit, influenced perhaps by Shakespeare's Sonnet 144 ('Two loves I have, of comfort and despair'). But he has already experienced the 'low beginnings of content' (lxxiv) and declared his heart cannot 'cannot rest quite in the love of what is gone' (lxxxv), as well as offered other less explicit suggestions that 'grief' is not what it was. So we reflect, at this stage, I think justly, that where there is room for fiction there is little grief; one has, as so often in this part of the poem, the sense of a routine reaction, a resort to 'regret' which is dramatically appropriate to a feeling partly cast off but for which no assured substitute has yet fully emerged.

No one will deny that this leaving Somersby and its associations is presented, and credibly, as an extremely painful experience. But what is also true is that it corresponds to and furthers glimpses of the change in the mind which have already been appearing for some time. Once that thread of association is broken, the way is clear for affirmation. This appears, as we have already seen, in the poems of the Third Christmas with their sense of strangeness mingled with a certain virtuoso spirit of good cheer. Here too appear the statements that sorrow may bring 'wisdom' (cviii), and here is rejected a transcendental faith – 'but mine own phantom chanting hymns?' (exaggerated in a plausible manner as necessarily 'barren' to this uncertain speaker trying to convince himself) – and asserted what is a true perception of 'grief' (though again rather impressively stated):

> *I will not shut me from my kind,*
> *And, lest I stiffen into stone,*
> *I will not eat my heart alone,*
> *Nor feed with sighs a passing wind.* (cviii)

Faith that Comes of Self-Control

As we have seen, the speaker in *In Memoriam* affects no great credence in the immortalising of Hallam or of his friendship in verse. He has little obvious belief in the poem as memorial, preferring to contrast such a function with a prime expressive need of his own. He imagines himself planting 'this small flower of poesy' on the tomb (viii). In a manuscript also[7] he developed the idea of rue, daisies, and 'sweeter blooms' for the grave, and in a highly artificial piece also omitted from the poem[8] he compares the merits of tears and 'trim-set plots of art' round the grave; but, though he longs to 'prove no lapse of moons can canker love' (xxvi), his general view is that memorials are small in the context of time – 'numb before the mouldering of a yew' (lxxvi). As Shakespeare contemplates transience in the image of the 'bare ruined choirs where late the sweet birds sang' (Sonnet 73), so Tennyson views his verses in the annals of time:

> *And if the matin songs, that woke*
> *The darkness of our planet, last,*
> *Thine own shall wither in the vast*
> *Ere half the lifetime of an oak.*
>
> *Ere these have clothed their branchy bowers*
> *With fifty Mays, thy songs are vain;*
> *And what are they when these remain*
> *The ruined shells of hollow towers?* (lxxvi)

Despite the professions of artistic modesty, the obstacles to immortality in *In Memoriam* are the same as the obstacles to immortality of any conception; transcendence appears a 'vacant yearning', a step of faith greater than reason will permit, and moreover one of doubtful practical value since there will still seem to be 'the reflex of a human face' (neither a perfect nor an imperfect transcendence will do); the alternative notions of subjective immortality in the mind or of preservation in art are alike subject to the impermanence and insignificance which appeared to be the lot of life in the face of the theories of evolution then in vogue; and the idea of immanence requires a more agreeable Nature than these theories seemed to suggest. To us the question of evolution may appear somewhat academic[9]. Yet the sense that the individual, as in Shelley's formation of 'that alone which knows' (*Adonais* 177), is lost in a huge and valueless flux is of deep concern in *In Memoriam*, and a sense that perhaps occurs more generally in our brave new world than we are always ready to admit. What is in question is nothing less than the existence of a soul which may be immortal and therein evidence its place in a scale of values and a universe with apparent purpose:

> *The wish that of the living whole*
> *No life may fail beyond the grave,*
> *Derives it not from that we have*
> *The likest God within the soul?* (lv)

Nature is first careful of 'the type', but 'carless of the single life'. In a later addition (lvi) Nature is equally careless of the type – there is no exception possible for 'man, her last work, who seemed so fair'. At this stage in the poem the answer is bewilderment. It is not accepted that this grim view of things can be correct, but neither is it denied. It is one with the 'grief' which governs the perception of reality by the speaker. The mystery is 'Behind the veil, behind the veil' (we recall the 'veil' image so frequently used by Shelley[10]), or

> *I stretch lame hands of faith and grope,*
> *And gather dust and chaff, and call*
> *To what I feel is Lord of all,*
> *And faintly trust the larger hope.* (lv)

Later, when the poem has begun to take a more optimistic turn, the answer is not essentially any different. There is a change of heart rather than any resolution of the conflict between knowledge and desire. But then the 'lame hands of faith' are less lame, and the speaker becomes able to see Hallam as representing, to mankind at large, what mankind at large represents to earlier phases of evolution – an idea which to the modern mind is perhaps more acceptable in principle than in detail, for Hallam has hardly been sufficiently characterised for us to believe that he might typify 'working out the beast' and letting 'the ape and tiger die' (cxviii). The view is that man is the 'herald of a higher race' and Hallam is a sort of prototype for the development.[11] The belief is a matter of subjective conviction, not in despite of the evidence (for Hallam is the evidence, though rather inadequately so in the poem) but because of it.

It is easy (and perhaps it is just) to criticise the licence provided by the creed of 'I have felt' (cxxiv). But we should beware of the grounds of our criticism. If there is a fault it is less in the notion as such than in the support which the poem may or may not give to it. For the credibility of the belief is entirely dependent on the values which Hallam has acquired in the poem and on the degree to which we feel able to respond to the growing light; the belief is the final manifestation of that light, not a stage in the argument, and the remaining parts of the poem are almost entirely celebration. Thus in the 'credo' (cxxiv) God and Hallam are connected by imagery, so that the 'infant crying for the light' (liv) and the hands of Hallam which have so often been sought, (particularly in the 'dark house' parts, viii, cxix), merge into a visionary contact and belief;

> No, like a child in doubt and fear;
> But that blind clamour made me wise;
> Then was I as a child which cries,
> But, crying, knows his father near;
>
> And what I am beheld again
> What is, and no man understands;
> And out of darkness came the hands
> That reach through nature, moulding man. (cxxiv)

It is a matter, then, of faith, but of faith which cannot be divorced from what the speaker has experienced. There is throughout the poem a distinction between 'faith' and 'knowledge'. The *Prologue* emphasises it from the standpoint of someone who knows the answers ('believing where we cannot prove'; 'We have but faith, we cannot know For knowledge is of things we see'), and at the end of the poem it has become something of a moral:

> With faith that comes of self-control,
> The truths that never can be proved
> Until we close with all we loved,
> And all we flow from, soul in soul. (cxxxi)

That is perhaps acceptable, provided we see it as entirely related to the dramatic structure of the poem; this is the conclusion of this particular speaker having done this particular battle with 'grief', and emerged with belief and self-respect ('self-control'). But as the 'moral' of the poet, of Tennyson, there is something slightly facile about it, particularly the closing lines, where 'close' suggests 'embrace' and the love of Hallam, but is vastly generalised, and where 'all we flow from' suggests *Adonais* ('but the pure spirit shall flow back to the burning fountain whence it came' – 338–9), whose resolution is of a somewhat different nature.[12]

We may feel the same of the *Epilogue*, where the poem's rather childless history of the relationship to Hallam is set in the context of marriage, of which it is held, after a rapid survey of evolutionary progress, that an offspring will be 'a closer link Betwixt us and the crowning race', with man 'no longer half-akin to brute'. Of this race, it is suggested in a peroration borrowed partly from Hallam's own writing[13], Hallam

> was a noble type
> Appearing ere the times were ripe,
> That friend of mine who lives in God,
>
> That God, which ever lives and loves,
> One God, one law, one element,
> And one far-off divine event,
> To which the whole creation moves.

It is not disputed that Tennyson in some measure believed this and that he associated the belief with the fact that through the loss of Hallam he himself had 'grown To something greater than before'. But it must on the other hand follow, from the preserving and 'weaving' of the whole cycle, that these 'songs' were in fact rather more than rejected 'echoes out of weaker times', and, whilst it is acceptable for what is virtually a new speaker to step in for the *Prologue* and *Epilogue*, it must be doubted whether the role of this speaker at the end of the poem itself is entirely happy. We witness a speaker growing to a sense of perspective and 'self-control' and we find that growth dramatically plausible. But when that speaker turns to address us in a rather more prescriptive fashion, and with an estimate of earlier productions which suggests a personality rather less than perfectly adjusted, we are apt to find the result unsatisfactory. We have the sense that the affirmations are endlessly repeated, even somewhat inflated against the now despised experience which, it is reasonably claimed, produced them.

The Mystic Glory

Reasons for a feeling of satiation before this pulpit are not hard to find in the differences between our own and the Victorian societies and conceptions of art. But there is another reason, and it is at the heart of the poem. Tennyson possessed, like Wordsworth, an abnormality of perception. Thus in the Fenwick note to the *Immortality Ode*[14] Wordsworth remarked:

> *I was often unable to think of external things as having external existence, and I communed with all that I saw as something not apart from, but inherent in, my own immaterial nature. Many times while going to school have I grasped at a wall or tree to recall myself from this abyss of idealism to reality. At that time I was afraid of such processes.*

Tennyson wrote[15]:

*A kind of waking trance I have frequently had, quite from my boyhood,
when I have been all alone. This has generally come upon me thro'
repeating my name two or three times to myself silently, till all at once, as
it were out of the intensity of the consciousness of individuality, the
individuality itself has seemed to dissolve and fade away into boundless
being, and this not a confused state, but the clearest of the clearest, the
surest of the surest, the wierdest of the weirdest, utterly beyond words,
where death was an almost laughable impossibility, the loss of personality
(if so it were) seeming no extinction but the only true life.*

There are similarities between these two accounts, although one implies
some sort of spontaneous exit from the self while the other speaks rather
of self-hypnosis. There is similarity, despite the great differences, also in
the poetry. In particularly, Tennyson shares, if less prosaically, what in
Wordsworth is rightly (if rather unfairly) characterised by Macaulay as a
'dreary wilderness of flat prosaic twaddle' surrounding momentary
perceptions 'into the life of things'. These momentary experiences are
inexplicable and even frightening, yet there is an urge to communicate
them. Therefore we find in the work of both poets instants of vision
surrounded by attempts at explanation and definition which are not the
less compulsively necessary because they are trying to put into words an
essentially physical sensation with, it is felt, more than physical implications.

The experience of a loss of individuality which reveals 'the only true
life' has a bearing on the nature of poetry as the speaker in *In Memoriam*
views it. That, as we have seen, is a rejection of 'parting and proving' in
favour of 'brief lays', expressions rather than disputations of 'grave
doubts and answers'. In all this the speaker has, of course, his dramatic
role to play, and no doubt the fragmentary nature of the whole may be
put down to his mental state. But, I think, only partly so; his insistence
on the instantaneous is due also to a conception of truth;

And holds it sin and shame to draw
The deepest measure from the chords;

Nor dare she trust a longer lay,
But rather loosens from the lip
Sort swallow-flights of song, that dip
Their wings in tears, and skim away. (xlviii)

Poetry, like vision, is as a flitting shadow or a ripple of water. It is
concerned with 'random influences' like light breaking on pools (xlix);

and the 'matured' and more authoritative speaker of the *Epilogue*, a longer and more ambitious piece, feels obliged to reject the 'brawling rhymes' of earlier days as 'the sport of random sun and shade' – as Tennyson came to distrust his 'vision', to depersonalise *In Memoriam* and to give elaborate explanations of its external structure which are hard to reconcile with the impressions which we receive.

But, though he rejects the earlier intuition, in favour of continuing his moral of 'progress', we can hardly reject it *in toto*. In fact the immense difficulty of framing the truth in 'matter-moulded forms of speech' (xcv) is central to *In Memoriam*. There are not wanting in the poem examples of experience akin to that which Tennyson mentions, and it is notable that they repeatedly adopt a special vocabulary to announce themselves as fundamentally indefinable. When the speaker 'seems to fail' from out his blood and 'grow incorporate with' the yew-tree (ii) we can hardly doubt that this refers to an abnormal experience, something more than a form of imagery, or that this loss of identity is related to the loss of ordinary reality as he stands outside the 'dark house' (vii), or the leaving his body for an hour in xii. More typically, the experience seems translated to the sphere of imagination (though we cannot tell), so that it occurs in a sudden inexplicably granted vision of Hallam or of union with him. For such insights Tennyson uses the words 'flash', 'mystic', 'wizard', or 'electric'. He wishes he could 'leap the grades of life and light And flash, at once, my friend, to thee', rather than be 'evermore a life behind' (xli) (By contrast, later in the poem he will welcome Hallam's advancement in the 'grades', his heralding of the crowning race.) He contemplates in the nightingale the mingling of 'fierce extremes':

> *And I – my heart would prelude woe –*
> *I cannot all command the strings;*
> *The glory of the sum of things*
> *Will flash along the chords and go.* (lxxxviii)

In an inverted, but still relevant, situation he wonders if Hallam, as one of the 'happy dead', will remember him in this way and have 'a little flash, a mystic hint' (xliv) of how things stand with those on earth. He is convinced that in a meeting 'I shall know him' and that, when they do part, 'We lose ourselves in light' (xlvii), and again, invokes him in his 'after-form' 'like a finer light in light' (xci). The walls of his room momentarily appear as marble in the moonlight, and the rays seem to carve an epitaph on this imaginary tombstone. When 'the mystic glory swims away',

> *then I know the mist is drawn*
> *A lucid veil from coast to coast,*
> *And in the dark church like a ghost*
> *Thy tablet glimmers to the dawn'.* (lxvii)

We may recall 'Death is a low mist which cannot blot The brightness it may veil' (*Adonais* 391).

Then again, if it is not by flashing light, it is by unearthly music that the supra-natural is recognisable. The face of Hallam cannot be accurately recalled,

> *Till all at once beyond the will*
> *I hear a wizard music roll* (lxx),

and the 'fair face' looks into his soul. In the vision of the great boat (ciii) as Hallam, Tennyson and the maidens turn towards their Wagnerian destination (the dream in part represents the idea of Hallam's spirit leaving Somersby and going with Tennyson to High Beech) in the 'crimson cloud',

> *the wind began to weep*
> *A music out of sheet and shroud.*

The image is repeated, this time with characteristic suggestions of a fast-beating heart, in cxxv ('Whatever I have said or sung'), where it appears to represent an appealing idea, a recaptured feeling, rather than an experience actually present:

> *Abiding with me till I sail*
> *To seek thee on the mystic deeps,*
> *And this electric force that keeps*
> *A thousand pulses dancing, fail.*

There is a sense in which (though Tennyson is more ambiguous on the theme even than Shelley) the 'kinship' of sleep and death is taken to represent the 'death' of this life compared with the reality to which Hallam might be presumed to have gone or, as in xliii ('If Death and Sleep be truly one') death itself is as a sleep,[16] we recall, from Tennyson's account, 'the loss of personality (if so it were) seeming no extinction but the only true life' and death as 'an almost laughable impossibility'. In that case death, which is but a prelude to the ultimate reawakening of 'the dawning soul', is as a 'trance' in which identity remains only as 'silent traces of the past', the 'colour' of some such closed flower as a tulip with the full brilliance within the folded petals. The hypothesis – and at this stage in the poem that is all it is – is a suspense of animation in which the identity is barely visible but remains as a 'figured leaf' to be 'unrolled' when the dead awaken. On the other hand, there is what appears to be the false simulacrum of this experience where it (or as it seems, the verbal creation of something like it) is the after-effect of stunning shock, a total confusion rather than an insight:

And stunned me from my power to think
And all my knowledge of myself;

And made me that delirious man
Whose fancy fuses old and new,
And flashes into false and true,
And mingles all without a plan. (xvi)

Here are the words of the visionary – 'fuses', 'flashes', 'mingles', but the words only, product of 'fancy'. 'Sorrow' or 'grief' is the 'changeling' which produces this muddle which is superficially so similar to the vision which can occur when grief is no longer 'clasped'.

It is plain that this unusual sensation, with its associated terminology, is particularly suggestive of the jumping of some bounds of normal knowledge, passing beyond the 'veil which those who live call life'. As such, its language is used in the effort to define what cannot be defined and in particular to weld apparent opposites into a unity recognised by a presumed higher perception. We have already seen the 'fierce extremes' admired for their fusion in the song of the nightingale, something which the speaker hopes is paralleled in his own poetry, which may 'flash along the chords' but which cannot be sustained – it will 'go'. In the later sections Hallam is repeatedly defined in terms of antitheses. He is 'manhood fused with female grace' (cix), 'so far, so near in woe and weal', 'known and unknown', 'human and divine' (cxxix), and he is, in the traditional comparison, 'Sweet Hesper-Phosphor, double name For what is one, the first, the last' (cxxi). He has not lost the 'traces' of individuality, but he also represents a whole, a totality. The speaker declares 'I mingle all the world with thee' (cxxix) and Hallam becomes 'mixed with God and Nature now'.[17]

But of course the 'fusion' or mergence which preeminently takes place is more comprehensive than the opposition of concepts to form a definition. It is the union of Hallam and the speaker, the joining of 'life' and 'death', which is seldom absent from the poem as a desire, occurs from time to time in what seems a conventional invocation and, more rarely, convinces us of a genuinely numinous perception which, for all we can say, may well have the meaning which the speaker, with dramatic propriety, asserts it to have. The difficulty, the inevitable prosiness or, which is as objectionable, prolonged poeticisms of stretches of *In Memoriam* is fundamental to its nature, though a realisation of that may not make these parts any more enjoyable. For this veridical experience has been hoped for and prepared for in hypothetical visions and forms of words. It has been glimpsed in what appears to be the fancy of the moonlight on the bed. It has been desired as 'to leap the grades of life and light And flash, at once, my friend, to thee'. All this is, as it were, preparation for the real thing, accompanied by moments of despair from which the brightest intuitions seem mysteriously to arise (a characteristic of elegies prior to their consolations, as we have noted). Yet this climax towards which everything moves is essentially incommunicable and indefinable, 'not a confused state, but the clearest of the clearest, the surest of the surest, the weirdest of the weirdest, utterly beyond words.' As the more 'moralising' and 'philosophical' passages which follow it are an attempted setting in context and interpretation, so what has gone before is one long preliminary, the elimination of absorption in the identified self of 'grief' so that speaker and reader are in a way hypnotised.

The climax, the vision which makes conceivable a consolation which, as in *Adonais*, is both immanent and transcendent, occurs in xcv ('By night we lingered on the lawn'), but it has been prepared for in the closely preceding sections, and in particular lxxxix ('Witch-elms that counterchange the floor'), where is described in a generalised, Augustan manner the bower beneath the sycamore at Somersby where Hallam is recollected to have read out the 'Tuscan poets' to a small gathering and where he and Tennyson debated the relative merits of town and country. This scene is perhaps the nearest to idealised pastoral that *In Memoriam* comes, and it has about it a strange, slightly unreal calm. We hear of their 'brushing ankle-deep in flowers', but the predominant mood is more that in the following lines;

> *O joy to him in this retreat,*
> *Immantled in ambrosial dark,*
> *To drink the cooler air, and mark*
> *The landscape winkling through the heat ...*
>
> *Nor less it pleased in livelier moods,*
> *Beyond the bounding hill to stray,*
> *And break the livelong summer day*
> *With banquet in the distant woods* (lxxxix)

(In other words, they went for a picnic.) There is something very civilised and also slightly outmoded about this, complete with its double negative, and the same is to be true of the climax, where this static pastoral is interrupted by incomprehensible experience.

Meanwhile, as if the speaker knows what is coming, there are invocations and speculations concerning the form of Hallam were he able to reappear:

> *Come, wear the form by which I know*
> *Thy spirit in time among thy peers.* (xci)

There are massive doubts also. 'If any vision should reveal' him, it would be 'canker of the brain' (xcii), purely subjective, or 'I shall not see thee' (xciii); but, as with *Adonais,* so much depends on what is 'he' – it might not be a 'visual shade of someone lost' which appears when (significantly) 'all the nerve of sense is numb', but rather 'he, the Spirit himself... Spirit to Spirit, Ghost to Ghost', and it is this which is invoked in 'Descend, and touch, and enter', these physical actions of so spiritual a being. Finally, there is a sort of purgation, a preparation of the soul:

> *In vain shalt thou, or any, call*
> *The spirits from their golden day,*
> *Except, like them, thou too canst say,*
> *My spirit is at peace with all* (xciv)

The setting of the visionary heart of *In Memoriam* is close to Hallam's retreat beneath the sycamore already mentioned, a tree which acquires a certain vague symbolic value (opposite to the yew) by way of this incidental association. As a composed, landscaped scene it is, in a sense, closer to pastoral than to Nature, but what is really distinctive about it is its neutrality, even objectivity. Nature is not here felt to be governed by the observer's perception or set down to provide a backdrop for the required mood of a poem; it has a solid, indubitable existence. The scene is of a summer night after a party. There are the characteristic descriptions of close detail – the bats

> *That haunt the dusk, with ermine capes*
> *And woolly breasts and beaded eyes* (xcv),

and the panorama – the songs pealed

> *From knoll to knoll where, couched at ease,*
> *The white kine glimmered, and the trees*
> *Laid their dark arms about the field.*

The members of the party retire into the house and the speaker is enveloped by that same 'solemn stillness' and prelusive darkness, 'the night in ever-nearing circle', that we have seen in the solitudes of Gray's *Elegy* and *Thyrsis.* He becomes, as in the description of his trance, 'all alone'. It is autumn and in the 'fallen leaves which kept their green', and more amply in the leaves of Hallam's letters which the speaker is reading,

> *strangely on the silence broke*
> *The silent-speaking words, and strange*
> *Was love's dumb cry defying change*
> *To test his worth...*

The sensation of communion is physical, correspondingly 'strange' because physical words cannot convey it, as if the letters are speech;

> So word by word, and line by lines,
> The dead man touched me from the past,
> And all at once it seemed at last
> The living soul was flashed on mine,
>
> And mine in this was wound, and whirled
> About empyreal heights of thought,
> And came on that which is, and caught
> The deep pulsations of the world.

An alteration in the text here is both interesting and insignificant. Depersonalising but also universalising the contact, Tennyson altered 'mine in his' to 'mine in this'; the emendation serves to draw our attention to the fact that either 'his' or 'this' will do, since it is the gist of this experience that 'The greater Soul may include the less'[18] and 'the loss of personality' seem 'no extinction'; Hallam, the One, essence, the speaker are for an instant all 'wound' together. But 'at length my trance Was cancelled, stricken through with doubt', a doubt analysed and finally defeated in the following sections, with the example of Hallam, whose religious faith had, while he lived, been a source of strength to Tennyson:

> Perplext in faith, but pure in deeds,
> At last he beat his music out. (xcvi)

After the entranced vision, the scene is frozen precisely as before, though now it is nearly dawn:

> Till now the doubtful dusk revealed
> The knolls once more where, couched at ease,
> The white kine glimmered, and the trees
> Laid their dark arms about the field (xcv)

As at the end of *Adonais* 'The breath whose might I have invoked in song Descends on me' (487–8), so a breeze begins to make the sycamore leaves tremble, gathers and rocks the 'full-foliaged elms', and announces the 'dawn', the mingling of 'East and West ... like life and death', the approach of 'boundless day.' The mingling of East and West is as the symbolic union of Hesper and Phosphor, Hallam in life and death;

> Sweet Hesper-Phosphor, double name
> For what is one, the first, the last,
> Thou, like my present and my past,
> Thy place is changed; thou art the same (cxxi)

If we have to find a single turning point for *In Memoriam* (which, mercifully, we do not) it is this vision, the change from 'the dead man' to 'the living soul'. It is here that the paradoxical fused opposites, so typical of the final sections of the poem, have their origin, and here, perhaps, alone that they fully convince. Such recited antitheses are, in effect, efforts to define this central experience, as so many of the earlier parts were attempts to reach it, which can scarcely be defined except in platitudes, so unsuitable are the 'matter-moulded forms of speech' (xcv). It is essentially the transcendent becoming immanent – though but for a moment 'utterly beyond words', yet to be related subsequently to ordinary life. It is only by this perception that the speaker is able to leave 'grief' without leaving also 'love', for the love is both beyond him in a spiritual world and yet able to be reached, proceeding as a 'diffusive power' into the whole of Nature. With the abandonment of 'grief', love becomes larger and more comprehensive:

> *My love involves the love before;*
> *My love is vaster passion now;*
> *Though mixed with God and Nature thou,*
> *I seem to love thee more and more.*
>
> *Far off thou art, but ever nigh;*
> *I have thee still, and I rejoice;*
> *I prosper, circled with thy voice;*
> *I shall not lose thee though I die.* (cxxx)

The Expressive Monument

I do not believe that *In Memoriam* has an intricate structure, that there is some 'key' as yet undiscovered. It is, as Tennyson asserted, a collection of elegies written at various times and 'woven' into a rough whole. There is no doubt that, as Tennyson declared[19] and Bradley elaborated[20], the three Christmases and recurring springs are major structural devices; they are fixed points at which progress can be reviewed by the reader and, as such, they are rather as a specific development of the elegiac convention of the 'the revolving year'. But that is not to say that the resulting divisions of the poem are clearly defined or that, for example, the sixth part after one Christmas will be notably comparable with the sixth part after another. There is no detailed, geometric plan of this sort. It seems rather that the time-scheme was imposed to compress the productions of a much longer period into a manageable fiction, which process has also the advantage of drawing attention to the ambiguity of poetic art with regard to autobiography; I put it that way because, whilst many of the lyrics present an imagined, fictional situation based on hypothesis (the speaker imagines, in his doubt, what it would be like if such and such were so . . .), while there is, particularly in the more self-pitying sections, an element of posturing hard indeed to distinguish from conscious ironic exaggeration, it is hardly the case that Tennyson strove very hard for anonymity, to encode references to the relationship of himself and Hallam – the inclusion of the reference to Hallam in the title (after the initial Trial Edition) shows the dilemma in which the poet found himself.

The idea of the speaker as an exemplar of a particular pattern of grief and recovery conceivably did not occur to Tennyson until the decision had been taken to weave the thing together, and indeed his own idea of this figure ('I' is not always the author speaking of himself, but the voice of the human race speaking thro' him'[21]) reads a little quaintly today. It seems clear that the *Prologue* and *Epilogue* (which were probably written in 1849 and 1844 respectively), with their references to a phase outgrown, postdate this decision and the emergence of the 'dramatic' concept of the speaker changing during the passing of less time than the dates of the poems themselves suggest.[22] Whatever we think of the two additions, they stem from a mental state, a detachment and enlargement, which could not exist whilst the state of 'grief' at all pertained. Whilst not necessarily direct expressions of the views of the poet in real life at these times or in general, they do represent a more abstract interpretation, a summing up from outside, of what has been seen actually happening within the poem. They might be viewed as a version of what we first saw in *Lycidas*, a comment by the poet on the views of the 'speaker' within.

This brings us to the final question, of where *In Memoriam* stands in relation to the tradition. It is an intriguing side-issue that the poem, though nearly furthest in date, is nearest in form to the original sense of 'eclogue' (a 'collection' or 'anthology'). But although its circumstances, of a sort of intermittent poetic diary juggled into a whole, are rather curious, it follows in outline the characteristic movement from absorption in mourning, through the examination of possible exits from the situation (a misery abhorrent as it is cherished), to a type of consolation which attempts to preserve the values recognised in grief, but also to make possible a fuller and more purposeful life. It also has the suggestion that the speaker in the course of expression discovers form, a discovery announced by a consolation in terms of which everything falls into place. Whether this is a fostered dramatic illusion or an accident in *In Memoriam*, it is typical of the monody on these themes. The work of art and the state of 'grief' are incompatible; the emergence of the one parallels the transcendence of the other.

With regard to pastoral, Nature is not idealised, partly because an idyllic past is less important to the speaker than the present state, and partly because it is doubtful until the end whether a predominant character can be attached to Nature at all whilst the speaker is preoccupied with subjective thinking and feeling. Nature is inclined to take on the moods of the observer, moods which by the end of the poem are felt to have misrepresented the Nature into which Hallam is now seen to be 'diffused'. Such a subjective distortion, inasmuch as it is recognised as a distortion, bears the relation of a simile rather than of a metaphor – Nature is felt to be *like* certain states of mind; that it actually mirrors them is a temporary misconception, as is the opposite idea (rarer in *In Memoriam*) that the state of mind is actually governed by the Nature which it perceives. Where spring contrasts with a wintery state of mind, it is the state of mind which governs the mood of the poem and what we sense as the true spirit of spring is derived, not felt. In *Adonais*, by contrast, there is a more equal clash between feeling and season (154–71). There is a reverse distortion in cxv ('Now fades the last long streak of snow') where there *is* a genuine creation of spring, and the notion that regret 'buds and blossoms like the rest' in this third spring strikes one as an artificial attempt to revive 'regret' when it is nearly dead. Now Nature is at last real, less dependent on the beholder, an influence against which he cannot long hold out – the evidences of spring

> *Cry through the sense to hearten trust*
> *In that which made the world so fair.* (cxvi)

For the most part, if he wishes to idealise the past, the speaker does so by highly artificial reference to 'Argive heights' and 'many a flute of Arcady' (xxiii), by the conventional 'path by which we twain did go' (xxii), or 'all our path was fresh with dew' (lxviii); they do not begin to ring true, and they are hardly meant to, for the speaker is scarcely able to suggest the quality of the past when he is so injured by loss. The pastoral convention is effectively rejected more firmly than in *Thyrsis* where it is felt to have at least a residual charm.

So far as a glorified pastoral 'bower' is concerned, there is no consistent setting for *In Memoriam*. The limitation is rather to an imaginary sphere of the mind in which are preserved, like the hallowed order of the pastoral world, ideas of love, grief and an afterlife which, whilst offering immortality, seems rather to increase than to lessen the gulf between the speaker and the beloved.[23] Because there is this absence of concrete location, of setting as real as the beholder, it is all the more striking that the vision of xcv ('By night we lingered on the lawn'), and the immediately surrounding parts, do take place in an enclosed pastoral world, namely the home at Somersby, which becomes substantial even as it has to be left. The portrayal is interesting. It is idealised in terms of a passing order, a settled community with the 'white kine' and the gracious trees spreading protective 'arms', not in terms of a Nature inspired by a vital force perceived by Wordsworthian insight. This, evidently, despite its prospect of fields outside and a 'bounding hill', is a landscaped, not a wild garden, with foliaged eaves and well-placed streams, a peace created, in part, by man. It seems to represent civilisation and is described in a calm and generalised manner suggestive of security and stability in the face of turmoil – notably, but not solely, the intellectual and emotional turmoil, as Tennyson finds it to be, of evolutionary thought.

It is in such a context that the vision which transcends the context occurs, and the fact of its occurrence, the immediacy of Hallam's presence in the ordinary setting (for Somersby, within respectable middle-class limits, is presented as unremarkable, unpalatial, and the 'diary' of poems has evoked humdrum life), suggests that its spirit is not only transcendent but also immanent. Yet it is, of course, a vision not tied to place and therefore, whilst the move to High Beech which follows it is a poignant wrench, the continuity survives and the implications of the vision can be explored as still meaningful when Somersby is, so far as the poem is concerned, forgotten.

Tennyson is not a 'nature poet'. Whatever conversion there is in the speaker, it owes very little to communion with Nature, even though a sign of its having occurred is his re-entry into harmony with Nature. He does not set any special value on Nature nor associate it with any single mood. The very mountains which the Romantics found symbols of mystery in permanence are for Tennyson representative of transience and passage – they are, ironically, as much 'seeming-random forms' (cxviii) as his verses seem 'the sport of random sun and shade'. He sets the whole in a context of flux too vast for the description 'pastoral' to be appropriate. Yet by the end of the poem Nature *has* an identity, as an order to which the speaker has adjusted and of which he is part. This quality is not independent of human activity, belief and feeling, but the speaker's greater breadth of view and acknowledgment of facts outside himself predisposes us to accept it as the more authentic view of Nature in the poem. It has, in this role, a certain composed and symbolic quality associating it with the world of Somersby, linking microcosm and macrocosm:

> And rise, O moon, from yonder down,
> Till over down and over dale
> All night the shining vapour sail
> And pass the silent-lighted town,
>
> The white-faced halls, the glancing rills,
> And catch at every mountain head,
> And o'er the friths that branch and spread
> Their sleeping silver through the hills;

And touch with shade the bridal doors,
With tender gloom the roof, the wall;
And breaking let the splendour fall
To spangle all the happy shore. (Epilogue)

This, we are to feel, is real, compared with the superb but ultimately fanciful lines of 'When on my bed the moonlight falls' (lxvii);

And then I know the mist is drawn
A lucid veil from coast to coast,
And in the dark church like a ghost
Thy tablet glimmers to the dawn.

The meandering of the early parts of *In Memoriam* represents, just as much as do the oscillations of *Lycidas* or *Adonais*, the mind distraught and seeking for a mode of coherent expression in which life's aims can be continued. In Tennyson's poem the matter is presented in terms not so much of the dedication of the artist and the destruction by an early death of the pursuit of true Fame – or even of unfulfilment, the leaf 'perished in the green' (lxxx) – as of the capacity to see any value and purpose whatever in the human world. Here *In Memoriam* may seem closer to a poem of its own time, like *Thyrsis*. *Thyrsis*, however, attains to a less optimistic stance (the possibility of a 'whisper') than Tennyson's speaker at a marriage ceremony, who celebrates the continuance of human progress while the proceedings are overlooked, in Hardyesque fashion, by 'a stiller guest, wishing joy', as 'the grave is bright for me' staying 'to share the morning feast'. Tennyson is again closer to Arnold in the relatively small tribute he pays to the beloved (partly because his qualities are regarded as indefinable) and the very great emphasis in the poem on the state of the person bereaved.

As memorial possibly created by the elegy itself, *In Memoriam* is notable for the low estimate of poetry (his own and in general) which the speaker claims to hold; this is something far beyond the modesty of Gray or of 'Moschus' saying his own verses cannot help Bion's cause with Proserpina. The assessment is no doubt due partly to the dramatic role of the speaker; he sees things this way because his mind is obsessed with another matter which must make all his efforts futile. But it is due also to the fundamental problem of conveying a crucial experience in words, and of suggesting that that incommunicable experience is of use to himself or to anyone else. The 'leap' from doubt to consoling faith is all the more difficult to imply because that faith springs from an experience of everyday life which is apparently little different from experiences when no such enlightenment occurred. But, reading the poem, we must surely sense that the self-doubt in respect of *In Memoriam* as monument is unwarranted.

133

It is a moving poetic statement of the values inherent in personal relationship, and of the problem of reconciling such values with human transience. It is an expression which has become the memorial of a possibility, a celebration of the refusal of man to resign those values in the face of death. It suggests the possible victory of love's 'cry defying change to test his worth' (xcv)'

NOTES

Introduction

1. Ian Jack, *English Literature, 1815–32* (Oxford, 1963), 90.

2. Brief summaries of the main elements in formal pastoral elegy are given by J. H. Hanford, 'The Pastoral Elegy and Milton's *Lycidas*', *PMLA* XXV (1910) 403–47, and G. Norlin, 'The Conventions of the Pastoral Elegy', *AJP* XXXII (1911), 294–312. A fuller survey is given in E. K. Chambers, 'The English Pastoral' in *Sir Thomas Wyatt and Some Collected Studies* (London, 1933), 146–80, and continuity with classical pastoral is also covered by W. P. Mustard, 'Later Echoes of the Greek Bucolic Poets', *AJP* XXX (1909), 245–83, and T. G. Rosenmeyer, *The Green Cabinet* (Berkeley, 1969), 112–25.

For historical stipulations as to the proper content of pastoral elegy, see J. E. Congleton, *Theories of Pastoral Poetry in England 1684–1798* (Gainesville, 1952); Pope's *Discourse on Pastoral Poetry*; R. Wallerstein, *Studies in Seventeenth Century Poetic* (Madison, 1950). Attitudes to literary genre in general are surveyed in R. Wellek and A. Warren, *Theory of Literature* (Harcourt Brace, 1949), Chap. 17, and Northrop Frye, *Anatomy of Criticism* (Princeton, 1957).

3. See B. Dobrée, *English Literature in the Earlier Eighteenth Century* (Oxford, 1959), 132–45.

4. 'Nature' and 'pastoral' are inevitably terms much used in this book and their definition is extremely difficult. In general, I use *Nature* to denote reality as opposed to pastoral and as the phenomenal universe, which may or may not include man, together with the elemental force presumed to drive it; and 'nature' for the conception (not entirely dissociated from the above) in which rural is opposed to urban life. The term *pastoral* is used of the literary image of an enclosed world, of which the Sicilian and Arcadian are examples. On the other hand, 'pastoral' is occasionally used to imply a contrast with a larger view of the human predicament represented by Nature (and is again not entirely distinct from the former sense). This 'pastoral' may be slightly disparaging and is very close to 'nature', but with more literary association; it is an impure form of *pastoral* – the convention without some of the impulse.

I have tried to maintain consistency in these usages, but of course there are difficulties when we distinguish our view or the reader's view from that of the poet, and the poet's from that of the speaker, and the point of a poem may be closely involved with such distinctions. For example, I do not think that Tennyson's characterisation of Somersby at the climax of *In Memoriam* will really fit any of these categories.

Chapter One – The Context

1. *Some Versions of the Fall* (London, 1973).

2. See, for example, W. Empson, *Some Versions of Pastoral* (London, 1935); W. H. Auden, 'Dingly Dell and the Fleet, in *The Dyer's Hand* (London, 1963), 409–15; Northrop Frye, *Anatomy of Criticism* (Princeton, 1957), Essay 3.

3. See also L. Lerner, *The Uses of Nostalgia* (London, 1972), Chap. 5 and R. Williams, *The Country and The City* (London, 1973), Chap. 3.

4. T. S. Eliot, *The Dry Salvages*.

5. On identification, cf. S. Freud, *Mourning and Melancholia* (1917):

> 'Profound mourning, the reaction to the loss of a loved person, contains the same feeling of pain, loss of interest in the outside world – in so far as it does not recall the dead one – loss of capacity to adopt any new object of love, which would mean a replacing of the one mourned, the same turning from every active effort that is not connected with thoughts of the dead. It is easy to see that this inhibition and circumscription in the ego is the expression of an exclusive devotion to its mourning, which leaves nothing over for other purposes or other interests'.

Freud describes 'an *identification* of the ego with the abandoned object.' *Collected Papers*, Hogarth Edition (London, 1925) IV, 153, 159.

Freud distinguishes 'mourning' and 'melancholia' by virtue of the 'loss of self-esteem' in the latter. The validity of the distinction in absolute terms is perhaps open to question but it is suggestive, although its application to literary portrayals is naturally complicated. Deprecation is a feature of both elegy and pastoral, but we may nonetheless feel that the 'grief' depicted in *In Memoriam* is close to what Freud meant by 'melancholia'. See also C. M. Parkes, *Bereavement* (London, 1972) 75, 90.

6. See particularly the consideration of these poems in D. Brown, *Thomas Hardy* (London, 1954), 170–83, and *Some Recollections by Emma Hardy*, ed. E. Hardy and R. Gittings (Oxford, 1961). Freud describes the normal process of 'recollection' as follows:

> 'The normal outcome is that deference for reality gains the day. Nevertheless its behest cannot be at once obeyed. The task is now carried through bit by bit . . . while all the time the existence of the lost object is continued in the mind. Each single one of the memories and hopes which bound the libido to the object is brought up and hyper-cathected, and the detachment of the libido from it accomplished . . . Reality passes its verdict – that the object no longer exists – upon each single one of the memories and hopes through which the libido was attached to the lost object, and the ego, confronted as it were with the decision whether it will share the fate, is persuaded by the sum of its narcissistic satisfactions in being alive to sever its attachment to the non-existent object.'

(*Mourning and Melancholia*, op. cit., 154, 166).

7. 'After a Journey' in *Collected Poems of Thomas Hardy* (London, 1930), 328. It is perhaps worth noting that the essential integrity and realism here are related in complex fashion to the 'pastoral' idealism of the last line, for that is a selective re-creation, if indeed it is re-creation rather than blurred vision.

8. Tennyson defined 'secular to-be' as 'aeons of the future'. This is a usage mainly of the 16th and 17th Centuries deriving from *L. Saecularis*, an age or generation.

9. 'Thou art indeed just, Lord' in *Poems of Gerard Manley Hopkins* (3rd. ed., Oxford, 1956), 113.

10. Spenser, *The Shepheardes Calendar*, 'November', 122–30.

11. Whatever the appropriate hour may be – for the propriety of Gray's ploughman in plodding his weary way at sundown has been challenged (see *The Poems of Gray, Collins and Goldsmith*, ed. R. Lonsdale (London, 1969), 116). Such mystery would, however, be typical of classical pastoral, where we are told nothing of the shepherds' lives away from the fields and may not even know whether they own their sheep or are employees.

12. *Theocritus, Bion, Moschus*, tr. Andrew Lang (London, 1892), 176.

13. Puttenham, in *The Arte of English Poesie* (1589) indicates the gist of much Renaissance discussion when he sees elegy as a sort of homeopathy whereby poets 'are as the Paracelsians, who were making one dolour to expell another, and in this case one short sorrowing the remedye of a long and grievous sorrow'. (*Elizabethan Critical Essays*, ed. Gregory Smith (Oxford, 1904), ii, 50).

14. *Lament for Bion*, tr. Andrew Lang, op. cit. 202.

15. *Lament for Bion*, see Note 14.

16. Keats, *Sleep and Poetry*, 101–2. The comparison of Keats's urn and Theocritus's bowl is developed by T. G. Rosenmeyer, *The Green Cabinet* (Berkeley, 1969), 91.

17. For a refreshing treatment of Virgil's *Eclogues* as pastoral, and of their allusions, see W. Berg, *Early Virgil* (London, 1974).

18. Marot and Petrarch had explored this technique, particularly for political and ecclesiastical matters, in an elaborate way. The relevant works are conveniently printed in *Milton's Lycidas*, ed. Scott Elledge (Harper & Row, 1966).

19. A succinct account of the problem is given in R. Wellek and A. Warren, *Theory of Literature* (Harcourt Brace, 1949), Chap. 7. For a vigorous attack in connection with Gray's *Elegy*, see F. H. Ellis, 'Gray's "Elegy", The Biographical Problem in Literary Criticism', *PMLA* LXVI (1951), 971–1008.

20. *The Letters of Matthew Arnold to Arthur Hugh Clough*, ed. H. F. Lowry (Oxford, 1932), 97.

Chapter Two – Milton – *Lycidas*

1. W. H. Auden, 'Robert Frost', in *The Dyer's Hand* (London, 1963), 340–1.

2. *The Early Lives of Milton*, ed. H. Darbishire (London, 1932), 54.

3. *Milton's Lycidas*, ed. Scott Elledge (Harper & Row, 1966), 141.

4. ibid.

5. The other elegists in the volume do, however, refer to his poetry (which consisted of Latin contributions to anthologies), and notably so Henry King (no relation), author of the *Exequy*, who wrote,

> He dresst the Muses in the bravst attire
> That ere they wore, and taught them a strain higher
> And far beyond their winged horses' flight.

6. Theocritus, *Idyll I*, 141 – ('The whirling wave closed over the man the Muses loved', in Lang's translation) – seems to have been in Milton's mind in his linking the death of the poet-shepherd by water to the floating of Orpheus's head (or Daphnis's body) 'down the stream'. The 'goarie visage' was originally a 'divine visage' – but that, perhaps, was unnecessarily to provoke a clash between pagan and Christian ideas already latent in the poem.

7. With 'strain of higher mood' compare Henry King's description of Edward King's poetic powers in Note 5 above.

8. W. Hall's contribution to *Justa Edovardo King* also has 'fatall bark'. But this was coincidence – there is no known evidence that the ship was at fault, and Hall does not use the same argument.

9. Whether the 'engin' will work by ecclesiastical reform or Divine Judgment, or both, has been much discussed. A summary of the views on 'this most debated crux in Milton' is given in *A Variorum Commentary on the Poems of John Milton* (London, 1972), ii (ed. A. S. P. Woodhouse and D. Bush), 686 ff.

10. 'Alph, the sacred river' of Coleridge's *Kubla Khan*, was believed to have flowed underground to join his beloved Arethusa in Sicily. The allusion to both may therefore represent a union of the peaceful pastoral of Theocritus with the more aspiring manner of Virgil.

11. See *Variorum Commentary* (above, Note 9), 722, for a summary of discussion.

12. A critical look at the earthly world is also not uncommon. The whole tradition seems to stem from Daphnis in Virgil, *Eclogue V*, who, apotheosised on the threshold of Olympus, looks down on the stars and clouds beneath.

13. It is with the arrival of Hesper, the evening-star, that Virgil's *Eclogue X*, the elegy for Gallus, ends, a conclusion that probably influenced that of *Lycidas*. In *Lycidas* it may be that the westering sun of the ending (rather than Hesperus) was imposed on Milton by his having used the 'day-star' for a special purpose in line 168.

Chapter Three – Gray –
Elegy Written in a Country Churchyard

1. Gray himself allegedly agreed that 'lacrimae rerum' would be a suitable 'motto' for the poem – see *The Poems of Gray, Collins and Goldsmith*, ed. R. Lonsdale (London, 1969), 113.

2. 'Yesterday I had the Misfortune of receiving a Letter from certain Gentlemen (as their Bookseller expresses it) who have taken the *Magazine of Magazines* into their hands. They tell me, that an *ingenious* Poem, call'd *Reflections* in a Country-Churchyard, has been communicated to them, wch. they are printing forthwith ... I have but one bad Way left to escape the Honour they would inflict upon me & therefore am obliged to desire you would make Dodsley print it immediately ... & the Title must be *Elegy*, wrote in a Country Church-yard ...' – Letter to Walpole, 11th February, 1751. (*Correspondence of Thomas Gray*, ed. P. Toynbee and L. Whibley (Oxford, 1935), i, 341–2).

3. *Correspondence*, ibid, iii, 1140.

4. W. B. Yeats, 'The Song of the Happy Shepherd' in *Collected Poems* (London, 1950), 7.

5. The *Sonnet* is 'problematic' in that it is hard to decide whether the artificial description of spring, to which the speaker is in his grief unable to respond, and to which we have also some difficulty in responding as it appears in the poem, is dramatically conceived or is a straightforward bid for Miltonic elevation (or both). The difficulty has some relevance to the *Elegy* and to Wordsworth's famous stricture that Gray was 'more than any other man curiously elaborate in the structure of his own poetic diction' (*Preface to Lyrical Ballads*), which takes his Sonnet as its text.

6. William Temple, quoted from Johnson, *Life of Gray*.

7. A summary, to which I am indebted, is given by Lonsdale, op. cit., 103–17.

8. I leave aside Mr Empson's well known criticism of these lines in the opening of his *Some Versions of Pastoral* (London, 1935). It does not seem to me that the flower's blushing is any more than a well-worn reference to its beauty of colour (and it is part of the point that this is *not* dependent in any way on the beholder). Neither does it strike me that the gem's indifference to being in a cave or the flower's aversion to being picked will make the images false for Johnson's 'common reader'; they may rather intrigue as pathetic fallacies. It is possible that 'by comparing a social arrangement to Nature he makes it seem inevitable, which it was not', but the feeling is surely that a particular 'social arrangement' is but an image of a large and less soluble problem related, as one might have expected Professor Empson to say, to the Fall. The 'lot' of the poor might be changed, but would they not then acquire the characteristics of 'the Proud'? To take this line is, it may be, to declare oneself the victim of Gray's self-deception or 'trick'; alternatively, it is to recognise with some humility the scope and sincerity of the poem.

9. William Mason, *Poems of Mr Gray* (York, 1775), 403.

10. See F. H. Ellis, 'Gray's *Elegy*, The Biographical Problem in Literary Criticism', *PMLA* LXVI (1951), 993.

11. See particularly O. Shepard, 'A Youth to Fortune and to Fame Unknown', *MP* XX (1923), 347–73. A selection of views on the subject is provided by *Twentieth Century Interpretations of Gray's 'Elegy'*, ed. H. W. Starr, (New Jersey), 1968.

12. The lines in *Lycidas* have been taken to be an invocation to the Muse to support the 'urn' or poem the speaker is making, but the explanation seems far-fetched and to violate the syntax.

13. Compare the end of Marvell's 'The Garden', where the soul has been 'at some fruit-trees mossy root':

> But 'twas beyond a Mortal's share
> To wander solitary there;
> Two Paradises 'twere in one
> To live in Paradise alone.

14. *Il Penseroso*, 'storied windows' (159), 'extasies' (165), 'pealing organ . . . anthems clear' (161), 'far-off curfew sound' (73), 'immortal mind which hath forsaken her mansion' (91–2), and 'th'accustom'd oak' (60) – are all echoed in Gray's *Elegy*.

15. Act II, Scene i, 30–2. The next line in the play refers to a 'sequester'd stag', cf. *Elegy* 75. Mason refers to Gray and Jacques as similar, see Lonsdale, op. cit., 136.

Chapter Four – Shelley – *Adonais*

1. See R. Langbaum, *The Poetry of Experience* (London, 1957).

2. W. H. Auden, *A Certain World* (London, 1971), 147.

3. Letter to Charles Ollier, 11th June, 1821, in *The Letters of Percy Bysshe Shelley*, ed. F. L. Jones (Oxford, 1964), ii, 299.

4. Letter to John and Mary Gishorne, 5th June, 1821, *Letters*, op. cit., ii, 294.

5. Letter to Horace Smith, 14th Sept., *Letters*, op. cit., ii, 349.

6. For Shelley's translations, see *Shelley, Poetical Works*, ed. T. Hutchinson (Oxford, 1967), 721–2.

7. Shelley had used the idea from 'Moschus' in *Lines Written Among the Euganean Hills* (1818), 183–8;

> What though yet
> Poesy's unfailing River,
> Which through Albion winds forever
> Lashing with melodious wave
> Many a sacred Poet's grave,
> Mourn its latest nursling fled?

Lycidas as the Cam's 'dearest pledge' (*Lycidas* 107) derives of course from the same convention.

8. *The Greek Bucolic Poets*, tr. J. M. Edwards (Loeb, London, 1970), 453.

9. Shelley had touched on the death of the gifted poet in *Queen Mab* (v, 127 ff,) which is much concerned with the search for lasting values in an unjust society, and for this passage he borrowed details from Gray's *Elegy*. Thus 'Penury' condemns talented beings to waste their lives in drudgery and the result is likely to be a 'rustic Milton' and 'vulgar Cato'. 'Cato' was originally proposed by Gray for the 'village-Hampden' of *Elegy* 57. In the letter to Horace Smith (see above, Note 5) Shelley asserts that 'I was resolved to pay some tribute of sympathy to the unhonoured dead', thus referring his purpose in *Adonais* to the speaker who is 'mindful of the unhonoured dead' in Gray's *Elegy* (93).

10. *Paradise Lost*, vii, 1–2: 'Urania, by that name If rightly thou art called'. The qualification recognises that this was not a regular usage but a transposition suitable to the start of an account of the Creation.

11. The comparison of thoughts to sheep, controlled by the self as shepherd, is a commonplace of Elizabethan pastoral, as is some uncertainty as to the nature of the controlling power. The most familiar example is Sidney's 'My sheep are thoughts', from *Arcadia*, where the shepherd both 'guides and serves' the thoughts. The idea of being at once

master and victim of a force was one which had a curious fascination for Shelley and is developed in his 'selfportrait' in *Adonais* 271–306.

12. The Dream, in saying (at this stage mistakenly) 'Our love, our hope, our sorrow, is not dead' (84) is echoing *Lycidas* (166) as a true immortality is announced – 'For Lycidas your sorrow is not dead'.

13. Edwards, op. cit., 393.

14. Ibid., 447

15. See Note 6 above.

16. Compare *Epipsychidion* 272–4, which was written at the same time. The poet-speaker, bereft of his divine love and inspiration, is described:

> Then, as a hunted deer that could not flee,
> I turned my thoughts and stood at bay,
> Wounded and weak and panting.

17. cf. *Lament for Bion*, 109–12 (the lines quoted by Shelley as the epigraph for *Adonais*); *There came poison, sweet Bion, to thy mouth, and poison thou didst eat – O how could it approach such lips as those and not turn to sweetness? And what mortal so barbarous and wild as to mix it for thee or give it thee?* (Edwards, op. cit., 453)

and *Adonais*, 316–8:

> Our Adonais hath drunk poison – Oh!
> What deaf and viperous murderer could crown
> Life's early cup with such a draught of woe?

18. For a discussion of earlier views on whether the dead 'sleep' (in the Christian context, until the Last Judgment) see H. Gardner, *Donne's Divine Poems* (Oxford, 1952) xliii–xlvi.

19. *Prometheus Unbound* (1819), III iv 190–3 and III iii 113.

20. See also Note 11 above. Sidney was no doubt in Shelley's mind because he had read Sidney's *Defence of Poetry* in connection with writing his own, three months before *Adonais*, in March 1821. Sidney died aged 32 of a thigh wound received in battle. Bion's Adonis was also killed by a thigh wound and the analogy was well drawn by the Elizabethan elegists of Sidney.

21. Lucan committed suicide at the age of 26 after entering a conspiracy against Nero, who refused to let him publish his poetry; his death is 'approved' because self-inflicted for the principle of free poetic expression.

22. The 'wedge sublime' is the pyramidal tomb of Cestius (as Shelley had written to Peacock). Its significance is in part that the memorial amounts to virtually the sum of knowledge concerning this Tribune; but for Shelley this ground is memorable as the burial place of his son William in June 1819, some two years before *Adonais*.

23. In *Lines Written Among the Euganean Hills* (331) Shelley writes of 'the frail bark of this lone being', with 'Pain' as its 'pilot', which is waiting for other tutelary spirits to guide it to a paradise far from 'passion, pain and guilt'. The 'polluting crowd' will not be there but, if they were, they would be converted.

Chapter Five – Arnold – The Scholar-Gipsy and Thyrsis

1. For a summary of the problems of dating, see *The Poems of Matthew Arnold*, ed. K. Allott (London, 1965), 331–2.

2. The analogy is of course a commonplace, but it is of interest that in 'Rugby Chapel' Arnold refers to his father as 'faithful shepherd' and to his pupils as 'sheep'.

3. Arnold has referred to a sequestered grange' shortly before – cf. Gray, *Elegy* (75), 'cool sequestered vale of life'.

4. *The Letters of Matthew Arnold to Arthur Hugh Clough*, ed. H. F. Lowry (Oxford, 1932), 146.

5. Ibid., 110.

6. Ibid., 71, and see L. Trilling, *Matthew Arnold* (1939, pb. 1963 London), 24–30.

7. See Notes 4 and 5 above.

8. H. F. Lowry, op. cit., 95, 128–31, 134–6. See also discussion of the poem in 'On Translating Homer' ('Last Words'), November 1861, where Arnold – as part of his review of Clough's achievement at the time (see Lowry, 158 ff) – praises rather Clough's 'Homeric simplicity' and the dedication to 'literature itself' than the qualities of the poem itself in detail.

9. See particularly K. Chorley, *Arthur Hugh Clough, The Uncommitted Mind* (Oxford, 1962).

10. H. F. Lowry, op. cit., 159 (Letter to Mrs Clough, 2nd December, 1861).

11. Although in *Thyrsis* he is criticised for deserting the Scholar-Gipsy, it is hard not to believe that Clough himself, in resigning from Oxford, was closely associated with the original Scholar-Gipsy of the imagination. Of Clough, as of the Scholar-Gipsy, it is true that he 'roamed the world' and in appearance came 'to little good'. His talents in fact were unfulfilled, but when he left 'with powers fresh', it must have been a matter of speculation as to whether he would make good. In fact, in Arnold's estimation, he did not. By the time of *Thyrsis* the myth is rewritten so that the Scholar-Gipsy's leaving Oxford is a minor matter compared with Clough's leaving what had been the source and meaning of the myth. The one is no longer a symbol of the other, and, since they began so close together, the separation of Clough and the Scholar-gipsy can be a little confusing in *Thyrsis*.

12. Tennyson was 24 when Hallam died in 1833, and he was 41 when he completed *In Memoriam*, so that the decline in friendship of Clough and Arnold with regard to *Thyrsis* is in part akin to the death of Hallam with regard to *In Memoriam*. In both, we have poets arrived at the maturity of their early forties and surveying an unforgettable attachment which was at its peak nearly twenty years earlier.

13. H. F. Lowry, op. cit., 130.

14. *Letters of Matthew Arnold, 1848–88*, ed. G. W. E. Russell (London, 1895) i, 327.

15. Arnold is inclined to see the fleeting lives and moods of man as sad and incomprehensible against a permanent cyclic Nature, thus suggesting something distinctly Victorian (even Tennyson is struck by the enormous continuity of Nature, though its evolutionary change baffles him) compared with the Romantic struggle to find transcendent permanence in a Nature of beautiful flux. Thus, in 'Resignation', dating from the 1840's, Arnold's speaker is struck by the contrast between life's unrolling,

> *A placid and continuous whole –*
> *That general life which does not cease,*
> *Whose secret is not joy, but peace* (190 ff.)

and the 'sad lucidity' of the observer conscious of the evanescence of human feelings –

> *The world in which we live and move*
> *Outlasts aversion, outlasts love.* (215–6).

17. The 'thorns . . . whiteblossomed' (113) may recall *Lycidas*'s 'first whitethorn' (48).

18. cf. Gray's *Elegy* (99), 'brushing with hasty steps the dew away'.

19. Lowry, op. cit., 111, 130.

20. See J. G. Frazer, *The Golden Bough*, Chap. 9.

21. *The Bhagavad Gita*, tr. J. Mascaro (Penguin, 1962), 56, 62.

22. Russell, op. cit. (see Note 14 above), i, 327.

23. cf. 'The Buried Life' (45–8)

> *But often, in the world's most crowded streets,*
> *But often, in the din of strife,*
> *There rises an unspeakable desire*
> *After the knowledge of our buried life.*

24. Lowry, op. cit., 159.

1. See Hallam Tennyson, *Alfred Lord Tennyson, A Memoir* (London, 1897), i, 305. This source is referred to below as *Memoir*. See also A. C. Bradley, *A Commentary on In Memoriam* (3rd edition, 1910), 67–8.

2. cf. T. S. Eliot, 'In Memoriam', in *Selected Essays* (London, 3rd edition, 1951), 332 ff: 'Tennyson is doing what every conscious artist does, turning his limitations (i.e. as a narrative poet) to good purpose . . . And the poem has to be comprehended as a whole . . . It is unique; it is a long poem made by putting together lyrics which have only the unity and continuity of a diary.'

3. *Memoir*, i, 304 and *Nineteenth Century* XXIII (1893), 182.

4. On the question of physical relationship, see C. B. Ricks, *Tennyson* (London, 1972), 216–9.

5. 'Thou art indeed just, Lord', in *Poems of Gerard Manley Hopkins* (Oxford, 3rd edition, 1956), 113.

6. *Memoir*, i, 72 and *The Poems of Tennyson*, ed. C. B. Ricks (London, 1969), 955.

7. *The Poems of Tennyson* (see Note 6 above), 914.

8. *Memoir*, 1, 306.

9. cf. R. Langbaum, 'The Dynamic Unity of In Memoriam' in *The Modern Spirit* (London, 1970), who finds the 'loss of faith' in Victorian literature may appear irrelevant to the modern reader who, according to Langbaum, very likely has had no faith to lose. Perhaps the best short account of Tennyson's attitude to evolutionary thought is in J. Kilham, *Tennyson and 'The Princess'* (London, 1958), 230–66.

10. See above, page 72.

11. The futurism here with 'Hallam' as 'herald' is reminiscent of Virgil, *Eclogue IV* (the so-called 'Messianic').

12. We recall that a slightly earlier part had seen Hallam overlooking chaotic revolution in a manner rather suggestive of the end of *Adonais*:

> *Whilst thou, dear Spirit, happy star,*
> *O'erlookest the tumult from afar,*
> *And smilest, knowing all is well* (cxxvii)

> *Whilst, burning through the inmost veil of heaven,*
> *The soul of Adonais like a star*
> *Beacons from the abode where the eternal are.*

> (*Adonais*, 493–5)

13. See *The Poems of Tennyson* (Note 6 above), 988.

14. *Lyrical Ballads*, ed. R. L. Brett and A. R. Jones (London, 1965), 286.

15. *Memoir*, i, 320.

16. See above, Chapter Four, Note 18.

17. cf. *Adonais* 370 ff – 'He is made one with Nature . . .' It is hard to doubt that Shelley's imagery in this stanza has influenced Tennyson's concluding sections, or that Shelley's neo-Platonic inferences were found conveniently to coincide with what Tennyson had to say of the transcendent spirit in immanent form as witnessed by his own 'mystical' experiences.

18. *The Poems of Tennyson* (see above, Note 6), 946.

19. *Memoir*, i, 305.

20. A. C. Bradley, *A Commentary on In Memoriam* (3rd edition 1910), 20–35.

21. *Memoir*, i, 305.

22. By the time of the *Epilogue* Tennyson seems to have been thinking of a whole and of the *Epilogue* as the end. Lushington declares that he said in the summer of 1845, 'I have brought in your marriage at the end of *In Memoriam* (*Memoir*, i, 203). This cannot be quite right, since the poem did not acquire this title until 1850, but presumably the drift is correct.

23. Speculations as to the nature of Hallam's 'after form' are a feature of the speaker's grief, which desires an immortality, yet not a remote one. The particular interest is in whether Hallam would be recognisable physically; 'a spirit, not a breathing voice' (xiii); 'wear the form by which I knew Thy spirit in time' (xci); 'eternal form shall still divide ... and I shall know him when we meet' (xlvii).

INDEX

Principal references are in italics

Actaeon, 68, 69, 75
Adonis, 9, 58, 59, 60, 62, 63, 67, 77. *See also*, Bion, *Lament for Adonis*
Alpheus, 33, 137n. *See also*, Arethusa
Aphrodite, 13, 60, 66
Arethusa, 25, 29, 33, 137n
Arnold, Matthew, 4, 13, 15, 19–20, 114; *Empedocles on Etna*, 81; *Resignation*, 141n; *Rugby Chapel* 146n; *The Buried Life*, 141n; *The Scholar-Gipsy*, 19–20, *81–9*, 90ff; *Thyrsis*, 13, 19–20, 80–1, *89–99*. *See also* Clough
'Artless tale', *see* Deprecation of art
Auden, W. H., 22–3, 29, 58
Auto-biography, *15–20*, 43, 48, 51–2, 55–7, 68, 81, 100–1, 121–2, 129–30. *See also* 'Dramatic' conception, Self-expression

'Bark', (ship as body), 29, 36, 75, 137n, 140n
Bhagavad Gita, 86, 96
Bion, *Lament for Adonis*, 9, 15–16, 58, 61ff, 65–6. *See also* Lament for Bion
Breeze, symbolic, 75, 128

Browning, Robert, 20, 56. *See also* Dramatic monologue
Bryskett, Ludowick, 10, 35

Cain, 68, 69, 75
Castiglione, 10
Christ, 36, 59, 68, 75
Clough, A. H., 13, 19, 81–2, *85–7*, *89–91*, 96, 98, 141n. *See also*, Arnold
Coleridge, S. T., 91
Consolation, 2–3, 6, *13–15*, 40, 60; in *Lycidas*, 35–6; in Gray's *Elegy*, 51–2; in *Adonais*, 63–4, 71–5; in *Thyrsis*, 92–3, 95, 97; in *In Memoriam*, 126–9. *See also* Memorial, Self-expression, Seasons
Cowley, Abraham, 24, 35, 79
Cowper, William, 59, 68

Death-wish, 2, 57. *See also* Identification
Deprecation of art, in *Lycidas*, 25, 37; in Gray's *Elegy*, 48–9; in *Adonais*, 76; in *In Memoriam*, 100, 102–6, 110, 133
Dome, in Shelley, 71–3
'Dramatic' conception, 3, *15–20*; in *Lycidas*, 27, 32–3, 37–9; in Gray's *Elegy*, 51–2, 55–6; in *Adonais*, 69–70, 76–8; in *The*

'Dramatic' conception—*contd.*
Scholar-Gipsy, 88; in *Thyrsis*,
91, 98–9; in *In Memoriam*,
100–6, 110, 121, 129–30, 133.
See also Auto-biography,
Dramatic monologue, Poet in
the poem
Dramatic monologue, 20, 56, 80,
101. *See also* 'Dramatic' conception

Echo, 60, 62
Eden, 1, 44, 49, 61, 139n. *See
also* Fall of Man
Elegy, varieties of, *1–21*, 22–3,
40–1, 81, 91, 96–8, 130. *See
also* Consolation, Memorial,
Pastoral elegy, Poet in the
poem
Eliot, T. S., 34, 136n, 142n
Empson, William, 1, 45, 138n
Evolution, 9, 110, 118–21

Fall of Man, 1–2, 44. *See also*
Eden
Fame, 11, 98, 133; in *Lycidas*,
28–9, 31–3; in Gray's *Elegy*,
44–6, 52. *See also* Memorial,
Unfulfilment
Flowers, 11; as consolation, in
Lycidas, 33–4, 39, 74, 98; in
Gray's *Elegy*, 50; in *Adonais*,
60–1, 74; in *In Memoriam*,
104, 113, 118; in flower pas-
sage, 33–4, 39, 93, 113, 118
Freud, S., *Mourning and
Melancholia*, 136nn

'Genius of the shore', 36, 51,
75
Glanvill, Joeph, 81ff
Golden Age, 1, 2, 57, 86–7
Goldsmith, Oliver, 79

Gray, Thomas, 1, 75, 79ff, 94,
95, 133; *Elegy Written in a
Country Churchyard*, 11, 17,
28, *40–54*, 55–6, 57, 139n,
140n, 141; *Prospect of Eton
College*, 47; *Sonnet on Death of
West*, 41, 43, 138n. *See also*
Autobiography, 'Dramatic'
conception, Social equality,
Solitude
Grief, 3–5, 136nn; in *Lycidas*,
22–3, 38; in *Adonais*, 4, 59,
63–4, 67–9; in *In Memoriam*,
4, 103, *106–18*, 125, 126, 129,
130. *See also* Re-creation

Hallam, Arthur, 9, 56, 90, 103ff,
119, 124ff, 132, *141n*. *See also*
Tennyson, *In Memoriam*
Hardy, Thomas, 3–4, 54, 114,
115, 133, 136nn
Hesper, 35, 74, 125, 128, 138n
Hopkins, G. M., 6–7, 114
Hyacinth, 29, 62–3

Identification, 3–4; in *Lycidas*,
26, 30; in Gray's *Elegy*, 49–50;
in *Adonais*, 59, 69; in *The
Scholar-Gipsy*, 82; in *Thyrsis*,
94–8; in *In Memoriam*, 127–
9

Jewel, image of, 28–9, 45, 48, 51,
138n
Johnson, Samuel, on Cowley, 24,
79; on Gray, 43, 47; on
Lycidas, 22–4, 29, 32, 36

Keats, 14, 15, 58ff, 80, 84, 91;
Ode on a Grecian Urn, 14,
137n; *Ode to a Nightingale*, 20;
Sleep and Poetry, 14, 15. *See
also* Shelley, *Adonais*

King, Edward, 10, 23ff, 137nn. *See also* Milton, *Lycidas*
King, Henry, 36, 137n; *Exequy upon his Wife*, 8, 11, 75

Lament for Bion, 7, 16, 33; in *Adonais*, 58–9, 62; Orpheus in, 12, 28, 93
Lushington, Edmund, 101, 108, 142n

Marot, Clément, 137n
Marvell, Andrew, *The Garden*, 2, 44, 139n
Mason, William, 40, 42, 43, 48
May Day, 31, 83
Memorial, elegy as, *10–11, 21*; in *Lycidas*, 25–6, 38–9, 105; in Gray's *Elegy*, 47–8, 52–4; in *In Memoriam*, 102ff, 118, 133–4. *See also* Self-expression, Tomb
Milton, *Comus*, 32; *Epitaphium Damonis*, 19, 24, 50, 92, 95; *Il Penseroso*, 44, 49; *L'Allegro*, 44, 49; *Lycidas*, 10–11, 14, 16–17, 19, *22–39*, 43ff, 51–2, 53, 70, 80, 84, 92, 98, 101, 105, 139n, 140n, 141n; *Paradise Lost*, 2, 139n. *See also*, Consolation, 'Dramatic' conception, Grief, Pastoral elegy, Poet in the poem, Priest-shepherd
Moschus, see *Lament for Bion*
Mourners, procession of, in *Lycidas*, 29ff; in *Adonais*, 67ff

Narcissus, 62–3
Nature, conceptions of, 2, *5–9*, 73, 110ff, 127, 130–1, *135n*; and evolution, 118–21; disjunction of mood and, 6–7, 93, 107, 110ff, 131–2; Nature mourning, 6–7, 24, 26–7, 33, 41, 62–3, 73, 93, 110; 'nature', 9, 15, 19–20, 57, 79–80, 83–4, 87–9, 97–8, 114, 132, 135n

Orpheus, 12, 13, 27–8, 48, 59, 93, 137n. *See also* Proserpina

Pastoral, conceptions of, *1–2, 5ff*, 28, 62, 65ff, *79–81*, 83, 89, 92, 104, 116, 126, *130–2*; rejected, 34, 63, 92, 111, 131–2. *See also* Nature, Pastoral elegy, Priest-shepherd
Pastoral elegy, conventions of, 1ff, 40, 67, 135n
Pathetic fallacy, 7, 138n. *See* Nature mourning
Persephone, *see* Proserpina
Persons addressed, in *Lycidas*, 34, 38; in Gray's *Elegy*, 17, 48–50; in *Adonais*, 57, 66, 70, 74, 77; in *The Scholar-Gipsy*, 82, 85; in *Thyrsis*, 20, 96–9; in *In Memoriam*, 18, 130. *See also* Auto-biography, 'Dramatic' conception, Poet in the poem
Petrarch, 137n
Platonism, 73–4, 76, 101–2
Poet in the poem, as subject, *10–12*; in *Lycidas*, 26–7, 29, 139n; in Gray's *Elegy*, 49–50, 54; in *Adonais*, 67–9, 76–8; in *Thyrsis*, 80, 98–9; in *In Memoriam*, 100–6, 130. *See also* Auto-biography, Self-Expression
Pope, Alexander, 13, 135n
Priest-shepherd, 30–3
Prometheus, 13, 62, 67

Proserpina (Persephone), 13, 14, 59, 93, 98, 133. *See also* Orpheus

Puttenham, George, 2, 137n

Reality, intrusion of, 3, 9, 27, 33–4, 38, 70, 84, 95

Recollection, Re-creation, 3–5; in *Lycidas*, 23–4; in Gray's *Elegy*, 49–50; in *The Scholar-Gipsy*, 80; in *Thyrsis*, 91–3, 98; in *In Memoriam*, 114–17, 126

River as mother, 29, 58, 139n

Seasons, 6–8, 60, 65, 93, 110–14; disjunction from, *see* Nature

Self-expression, consolation in, *11–12*, *14–15*, *17–21*, 23–5, 100, 102ff, 130–4. *See also* 'Dramatic' conception, Memorial

Shakespeare, 49; *Sonnets*, 11, 117, 118

Shelley, *Adonais*, 1, 4, 14, 18, *55–78*, 82, 84, 87, 93, 107, 110, 119, 120, 124, 128, 140n, 142n; *Defence of Poetry*, 61, 75, 78; *Epipsychidion*, 140n; *Lines written among the Euganuan Hills*, 139n, 140n; *Mont Blanc*, 71–2; *Prometheus Unbound*, 140n; *Queen Mab*, 63, 139n; *The Sensitive Plant*, 72

Sidney, Sir Philip, 74, 139n, 140n

Sleep, death as, 44, 53, 62, 65, 71–2, 124, 140n

Social equality, in pastoral, 1; in Gray's *Elegy*, 44–6, 52–4, 138n

Solitude, 1, 43–4, 45–6, 56, 75, 83, 96–8, 127, 139n

Spenser, *The Shepheardes Calendar*, 16, 30–2, 37

'Stain' image, 72–3, 87

Star image, 67, 75, 142n. *See also*, Hesper

Tennyson, *In Memoriam*, 5, 7ff, 15, 18, 40, 43, 50, *100–34*; faith and knowledge in, 118–20; grief in, 4, 12, *106–18*; move from Somersby in, 116–17, 124, 132; evolution in, 118–21; pastoral in, 116, 127, 130–4; structure, 100–1, 129–30. *See also* Visionary experience. *Ulysses*, 56

Theocritus, 2, 27, 32, 33, 40, 57; *Idyll I*, 13ff, 27, 137n

Time, 3–5. *See* Seasons

Tomb, decking of, 10, 21, 34, 35, 38–9, 74, 104. *See also*, Flowers, Memorial

Tree, favourite, 49, 50, 91–7, 126–7

Unfulfilment, 8, 28, 51ff, 74, 90, 98, 133. *See also*, Fame

Urania, 59–60, 62, 66–7, 69, 104, 139n

Veil image, 71–2, 75, 119, 123–4

Vesper, *see* Hesper

Virgil, 29, 33, 57, 87, 137; *Eclogues* (II) 50, (IV) 33, 92, (V) 10, 13, 17, 138n, (VII) 93, (IX) 19, (X) 14, 25, 27, 138n

Visionary experience, of Tennyson, 111, *121–9*; of Wordsworth, 121–2

Walpole, Horace, 42, 49
West, Richard, 41ff, 51ff
'Where were ye?' formula, 14,
27, 60

Wordsworth, 79, 91, 121–2, 132,
138n

Yeats, W. B., 41